Book Description

Do you treat everyone with equal a everyone with equal amounts of res on.

Do you have good manners, or good fucking manners? Have you ever thought that the manners you were taught are fucktarded? Do you not trust polite people? Wonder if there's a correct way to be mean? Want to remake yourself into a paragon of efficiency, transparency, and good fucking manners? Then this is the etiquette book for you! The Juice Nazi and his Head of Secret Police, Roxanne G., are back, angrier than ever and ready to impose their will on dipshits who dare oppose them. In this book, they dissect American middle-class manners to reveal an etiquette system rife with genteel bullying, moral grandstanding, and narcissistic delusions. They offer, in its place, an alternate etiquette system that doesn't tolerate anything that's fake, senseless, and wasteful. This book profanes the sacred and will make anyone who identifies as a middle-class American in morals and manners, squirm. Misanthropists will be delighted.

Contents

Introduction

Most people think they have good manners. Most of these people are wrong, they don't know jack shit about good fucking manners.

To begin with, anyone who thinks good manners is about following a set of arbitrary and sometimes asinine procedures is a boorish ninny who can't think. One can't be well mannered without having considered the meaning and purpose behind and effectiveness of each action, okay? Well-mannered people are *aware* – they're sensitive to context and purpose – and they're curious. It's the insolent and lazy who use the same pick-up lines regardless of the situation, despite consistently obstructive consequences. It's the awkward and brainwashed who can be convinced that bitch slapping someone can be a polite greeting in another culture, just because the ethos of multiculturalism says so. These are the people who take up two parking spots and aren't paying attention when the light turns green.

One needs to understand why "good manners" are good manners to be well mannered. If you don't wonder why a certain act is "good," then there's a swell chance you have bad manners because etiquette is often slow to adapt to the changing world. For instance, what's the point of the handshake? Are we showing that we aren't carrying a dagger, that we come in peace? Is it still more egalitarian and warmer than tipping the hat (that few wear nowadays) and curtsies, as the Quakers believed? Does the transfer of germs make more people sick, or does it facilitate herd immunity? Will the handshake survive the 2020 pandemic? Should it?

What's the purpose of having good manners and what's its relationship to etiquette? From what I've seen, most of the Anglo cultured world equate "good manners" with one's knowledge and ability to follow prevailing etiquette. In other words, "good manners" is a matter of social access and the implication is that it's the upper class that determines the codes of good conduct. Here's a definition of etiquette from Merriam-Webster dictionary that reflects that ethos:

> *the conduct or procedure required by good breeding or prescribed by authority to be observed in social or official life.*

Etiquette here is delineated as a top-down mechanism, "prescribed by authority," and/or by those of "good breeding," which I take to mean the upper class. Not all dictionaries agree with this definition, let's look at Oxford Language's more egalitarian definition of etiquette:

> *the customary code of polite behavior in society or among members of a particular profession or group.*

This definition implies that each social class has its own set of rules and none are intrinsically superior to others. And these codes can be developed organically, bottom-up, rather than from sources of authority.

This tension between egalitarianism and elitism pervades American social life, resulting in ludicrous habits that get passed off as "good manners." So many Americans – left-wing Americans especially – want it all, they want to stick up for common folk AND be recognized as elite, which is why they're called champagne socialists, or limousine liberals. This paradox results in an etiquette system that encourages manners that are fake, senseless, and wasteful. Parodies, really, performed by people who act and sound like muppets.

It doesn't have to be that way. The aim of this book is to suggest an alternate etiquette system that encourages people to be authentic, transparent, and efficient. The basis of this etiquette system – Part I of this book – is the title of the first chapter, *Don't Waste People's Time.* Well-mannered people don't show off their good breeding – that'd be narcissism at work and it's a waste of time – they're focused on making their own and other people's lives better and easier. This chapter also explores why so many Americans think it's good manners to waste people's time. Chapter 2 is a test of how well-mannered you are in the alternate etiquette system proposed in this book.

Part II is about the *Secondary Principles* one should abide by to be well-mannered. These include: *Save Other People Time*, the title of chapter 3. To do so, *Don't Lie*, the title of chapter 4. Yes, not lying will hurt people's feelings, but well-mannered people care more about truth than feelings, and worrying about people's feelings is a waste of time. Good news is that not lying doesn't mean you have to say anything. So we segue to chapter 5, *Less is Best*, which shows you how to be minimalistic in interactions so you don't say something stupid. Doing so will save you and others time. *Show, Don't Tell* is the title of chapter 6. Well-mannered people say less and do more because actions and results mean more than words. In chapter 7, *Treat Others as They Treat You*, elucidates the difference between empathy and sympathy and explains why treating others as you want to be treated is a narcissistic act that'll get you in trouble.

Part III, *Situations,* applies the above principles to specific situations. Chapter 8, *Phone Etiquette*, shows the proper way to place a call and answer them. This is especially important if you're in sales, good phone etiquette will increase your sales, guaranteed, or Dipshit Doug Evans Dickhead will grow a dick that's not on his head. Chapter 9, *The Art of Being Mean*, explores how to be mean to someone with style so you don't look like a dipshit dickhead. We pivot to *Be Kind, Not Nice* in Chapter 10 because so many people who think they're being nice are actually acting like a Dipshit Doug Evans Dickhead. Chapter 11, *Awkward Situations*, shows you how to act gracefully when the situation gets weird. *Restaurant Etiquette* is the subject of Chapter 12, so you don't dine like a Dipshit Doug Evans Dickhead when you're eating out. Chapter 13, *How to Talk to Customers* puts the principle "Treat Others as They Want to

Be Treated" in action. Those in the service industry should read this chapter. In Chapter 14, *Bad Manners* that rarely get called out are discussed and dissected to reveal an American culture with fucked up priorities. It also shows you how to respond to bad manners with good fucking manners. Touché, villains!

Part IV examines the *Purpose of Good Fucking Manners*. Like, what's the point of this book and what can you do with it? Chapter 15 elucidates why *Chinese People Don't Say "Thank You"* anywhere as often as Americans do. Is it because the Chinese are rude? What does it say about the philosophical underpinnings of Chinese society? What does this contrast reveal about American society and manners? This chapter de-normalizes American notions of what is proper. Chapter 16 is a review of famed chef Marco Pierre White's memoir: *Devil in the Kitchen*. What sort of manners did he have to become the youngest, at age 33, to win three Micheline stars, become the first TV rockstar chef, and train famous chefs such as Gordon Ramsey, Heston Blumenthal, and Mario Batali? More of the same in Chapter 17, except here it's about *How Steve Jobs Made Your iPhone*. Did Steve Jobs have good manners, or good fucking manners to make his vision reality? In Chapter 18, we appraise the *Purpose of Good Fucking Manners*. What can you achieve with good fucking manners, assuming you don't find it revolting? Chapter 19 introduces some of you to *Suggested Readings* that have shaped this book. These include etiquette classics by Emily Post, Amy Vanderbilt, and Miss Manners; lesser-known ones by outlandish authors such as flaming fag Quentin Crisp and the "Queen of Mean," Florence King; and well-known authors whose books can be read as, but aren't, about etiquette, such as Robert Greene and Friedrich Nietzsche. This chapter conveys that there are divergent thoughts about etiquette and it's up to you to decide what works best for you.

We finish with *Final Thoughts and Questions* in Chapter 20, where I talk about my transcultural experiences with etiquette to highlight the uniqueness of American preoccupation with etiquette and of its implications. I also ask the reader questions about their relationship with etiquette. Do you respect everyone equally? Should you?

After you've read the first seven chapters, you can skip around. You need to understand the principles behind my etiquette system before you can understand how they work in everyday situations.

Send comments, including hate mail and death threats, to foodyap@gmail.com. Write in the subject line: Dipshit Doug Evan is a Dickhead and we'll get back to you. Enjoy!

If you want to ask Dipshit Doug Evans why he's such a dickhead, his e-mail is doug.evans419@gmail.com. If you want to ask his mom why he's a dipshit, e-mail her at stardust71@gmail.com.

Part I
Basis of Good Fucking Manners

In social matters, pointless conventions are not merely the bee sting of etiquette, but the snake bite of moral order.

– Florence King, from *Lump It or Leave It (1990)*

Chapter 1
Don't Waste People's Time.

The cornerstone of good fucking manners is *don't waste people's time*. That's it. Good fucking manners have nothing to do with overwrought rituals such as saying "please" and "thank-you" when asking for or receiving something, or asking vapid questions like "how are you" when you really mean to say "hi" or nothing at all. In fact, the incessant mutterings of "thank you" during a simple transaction are signs of someone who is incompetent, socially inept, and vile in character. Beware, it's like being love bombed, there's a dark side to so much cheap effort used to announce one's good manners and intentions. One "thank you" per transaction is enough.

What's the big deal about time? After all, the value of time is subjective. For productive people, time is the most valuable commodity in the world because our time in this world is limited. The lazy, most of them prefer to not make a big deal about time, they don't like to be rushed. So why build an etiquette system around time when many people don't value it?

I don't want to be poor or live in a poor nation. The Philippines is poor because of "Filipino time" – Filipino carelessness regarding time – yes?[1] Black Americans are poor because of colored people's time, maybe? Time obsessed Germans and Swiss are wealthier than the Italians and Spanish, who have a more relaxed attitude toward time. My Greek-American friends tell me that all the hard-working and time conscious Greeks leave economically struggling Greece because they can't stand how irresponsible most Greeks are with time.

---

[1] Search for "Filipino time" and "are Filipinos lazy" for lay and academic perspectives on stereotypes about Filipinos.

So the etiquette system I propose isn't meant to be universal. It's meant to accommodate productive and ambitious people, to help them maximize their output by removing senseless barriers that waste their time. The parasites of society can continue on as they wish and the rest of society will have to work around them.

What Happens When We Focus on Not Wasting People's Time?

That's how we show respect to other people – the unproductive included – by caring about their time. We show up on time to not keep them waiting. We don't say more than necessary. We don't ask stupid questions if we're not interested in hearing an honest answer. So we say "hi" instead of "hi, how are you?" when we're not interested in how someone is. And we never waste our breath on dishonest answers such as "I'm fine" when we're anything but. We eliminate information that's unnecessary, the kind of stuff that probably makes us look defensive, pompous or whiny. For instance, I once received an email telling me someone had died. It began with:

> *It is with a heavy heart and deep sadness that I announce that so and so has died.*

Which makes the sender sound like a pompous narcissist – look at me, look at how sentimental I am about so and so dying. Is the subject the person who died, or the person announcing the death? Just say what needs to be said:

> *So and so died.*

Because that's all people need to know, they don't need a daytime drama sideshow to go with it.

Here's another example of someone saying too much after being reprimanded for putting something highly flammable near flames.

That's the only time I've done that.

She sounds defensive. Which means that she has likely done that before and will do it again, her defensiveness prevents her from learning from her mistake. Narcissism, not ignorance, is why history repeats itself no matter how much it's studied. "If my friends and I ran a Socialist nation, it'd work out this time without bloodshed," thinks the maudlin Political Science major after reading his *Marx and Engels Reader,* "because I've read about the mistakes made in the past." Or check the meth and heroin relapse rates at the best recovery centers, ~ 80% relapse.[2] What she should say if she wants to stop fucking up:

Ok, sorry.

Not being defensive is the first step toward stopping a bad habit. Defensiveness is the inflated ego protecting itself and is the source of most wasted time.

Which brings us to the most important effect of not wasting other people's time – it discourages using manners as an expression of one's "good breeding" because you're focused on *other people* and *their* time instead of your image. Every moment spent embellishing one's image for all to admire is a waste of people's time. Most people don't give a shit about your image, they mostly care about their own image and what

---

[2] From *10 most common reasons people relapse,* found on https://www.familyaddictionspecialist.com/blog/10-most-common-reasons-for-addiction-relapse
"Unfortunately relapse rates for individuals who enter recovery from a drug or alcohol addiction are quite high. Studies reflect that about 40-60% of individuals relapse within 30 days of leaving an inpatient drug and alcohol treatment center, and up to 85% relapse within the first year."

they can get from you. That's why productive people aren't distracted by status, they're focused on truth, action, and results. Get the ego under control to get those results.

Why Americans Talk So Much

Because many of them are pompous fucktards in love with the sound of their own voice, according to grumpy social critic and literature professor, Paul Fussell. Middle-class Americans are the worst, he says, and they mistake verbosity for signs of intelligence and avoidance of the unpleasant for good breeding.

> *The middles cleave to euphemisms not just because they're an aid in avoiding facts. They like them also because they assist their social yearnings towards pomposity. This is possible because most euphemisms permit the speaker to multiply syllables, and the middle class confuses sheer numerousness with weight and value.[3]*

For Fussell, American manners are invariably and uncomfortably a matter of class. Especially for the middles, and it's precisely their obsession with status and being liked that makes them insufferable. Fussell invokes Lord Melbourne:

> *The higher and lower classes, there's some good in them, but the middle classes are all affectation and conceit and pretense and concealment.[4]*

That's because the middles, poised between what they consider the unattainable upper heaven and the encroaching prole abyss, are insecure.

---

[3] Paul Fussell (1992). "Class: A Guide Through the American Status System", p.160, Simon and Schuster

[4] Ibid.

Fussell regards them as cogs in America's corporate machine – interchangeable and unsettled, thus subject to "status panic" expressed by putting on airs to hide their anxiety. So it's among the middles that we see "good manners" – genteel bullying, moral grandstanding, and narcissistic delusions. So delusional that I bet the American middle-class are the most medicated demographic in the history of the world. Practicing "good manners" isn't healthy, if you need another reason to adhere to an etiquette system that focuses on not wasting other people's time with social self-preening.

The uppers are self-assured, that's why they're cool and like some freaky shit. The lowers don't give a shit, that's why they're fun and why they make some freaky shit. The middles, in contrast, strive to be as inoffensive as possible, they just want to be liked and admired. Which, ironically, makes them offensive to all leading etiquette experts I've read to write this book and especially to Fussell. Seeking self-improvement and refinement, the middle class "opts for the showy, and in so doing takes a pratfall."[5] Fussell holds them responsible for debasing the English language by adding unnecessary syllables in hope that they'll confer added dignity and worth. "Can you please pass me the salt, if you don't mind?" is an example of middle-class good manners that's irritating as fuck because it's a waste of time. "That book was rather good" is another one. But where middle-class "good manners" become dangerous – see the havoc the pc language police have created – lie in its aversion to "sharp meaning" and "disinclination to accept unpleasant facts."[6] This is where you get lies to protect and/or inflate the ego. The Subway grunt is a "sandwich artist." The secretary is a "project coordinator." The shopkeeper is a fucking "CEO." This is also where you get dangerous white lies that keep people from confronting reality about the world. "Quantitative easing" for printing money out of thin air. "Inner city" for slums. "Peacekeeping" for invasion. Fussell calls this garbage "jargon,

---

[5] Ibid.
[6] Paul Fussell (1991) *BAD or, The Dumbing of America*

gentility and verbal slop."[7] I agree, and people go crazy when they don't see themselves and social reality with honesty and clarity.

Etiquette isn't something to be respected and blindly accepted as is. Etiquette should always be studied and critiqued because that's where we'll see, in plain sight, society's perversions, travesties, and paradoxes. ...scribble page!

---

[7] Ibid.

Chapter 2
Good Fucking Manners Test

Take this to see if you have good manners or good fucking manners. Answers at the end.

1. You're at dinner and want someone to pass you the salt. What do you say?
   a) Can you please pass the salt, when you get a chance?
   b) Pass the salt.
   c) Pass me the salt now or I'll hit you.

2. You're making a sales call. How do you greet the person you're calling?
   a) This is so and so calling from such and such business. Can I speak to so and so?
   b) Hi, how are you today?
   c) Hi, can I please speak to so and so?

3. You're a host at a restaurant. How do you greet a customer?
   a) Hello sir, how are you this lovely evening?
   b) How many?
   c) Hi, how are you?

4. The grocery clerk greets you: "Hi, how are you?" How do you respond?
   a) I'm fine, thank you. How are you?
   b) Busy.
   c) None of your business.

5. Light turns green but the car in front of you doesn't move. What do you do?
   a) Hand on horn until this dipshit moves.

b) Don't do anything.

c) Tap on the horn.

6. Car behind you honks because the lights green and you're stalled. What do you do?

a) Drive and give finger to honker.

b) Drive.

c) Wait until light turns yellow, then go.

7. Your daughter loves gymnastics and is about to enter her first meet. She's confident about winning and even thought about the perfect place to hang her blue ribbon. While she did well, she didn't medal, and was devastated. What do you, as a parent, tell her?

a) Tell her you thought she was the best.

b) Tell her she has the ability and will surely win next time.

c) Tell her she doesn't deserve to win because she didn't work hard enough.

8. Customer is angry about something. How do you make him less angry?

a) Tell him to calm down, everything will be fine.

b) Be upset about what the customer is angry about.

c) Look concerned and distressed.

9. Your partner tells you you're lazy. How do you respond?

a) Takes one to know one, asshole.

b) Why am I lazy?

c) You never see all the things I do for you.

10. Traffic is worse than usual, so you're 15 minutes late to work. What do you say when you show up?

a) Sorry I'm late, traffic was awful, I've never seen it this bad.

b) Sorry I'm late.

c) Sorry I'm late, someone spank me.

11. Manager points out the mistake you made. What do you say?
   a) Shit, sorry.
   b) Sorry, this was the first time I made the mistake.
   c) But it was really busy.

12. You get stopped for speeding. Officer asks you where you're going. How do you respond?
   a) It's dark, I can't see the speed limit sign and I'm already late for work!
   b) I'm sorry for speeding but I'm late for work and I really can't afford a speeding ticket right now.
   c) Work.

13. Co-worker put something in the wrong place. Manager asks you why it's there. What do you say or do?
   a) She put it there, I didn't do it.
   b) Move it to the right place.
   c) I have no idea how it got there.

14. How do you tell employee about a mistake they made?
   a) You're a great guy but your calculations here are wrong. Can you fix them, if you don't mind? You're a great team player, btw.
   b) These are wrong, fix them.
   c) I know this sounds harsh and I don't mean anything personally, but can you look over these calculations again?

15. As you're focused on a complicated order, condescending customer tells you that you should smile more if you want a tip. How do you respond?
   a) "I'm sorry, I'm having a bad day.
   b) Smile more.

c) Ask her if she'd like a side order of "Fuck Off" to go with her order.

16. What do you say or do to mother whose daughter is throwing ice cubes at other customers?
    a) Madam, can you please stop your daughter from throwing ice cubes, if you don't mind.
    b) Throw ice cubes at them.
    c) Tell her to get the fuck out.

17. Customer asks for something that's not on the menu. What's your response?
    a) No, we don't have that.
    b) Restaurant down the street has that, go there.
    c) We have something similar, want to try it?

18. Your 8-year-old is new at school. He gets shoved out of lunch line and is told to get to the back. He responds by beating the shit out of the kid who bullied him. What's your response?
    a) Ground him and make him apologize to kid he beat up.
    b) Tell him he did the right thing and to never worry about lawsuits, you'll take care of those if they come up.
    c) Have your kid apologize to the kid he beat up and have them talk it out. End with hug.

19. Earthquake during math class! Big enough to topple bookshelves. Nobody is hurt, everyone is okay, just jittery. What do you, as teacher, do?
    a) Stop class, act jittery and anxious because that's how you feel.
    b) Have students clean up mess and continue class as if nothing happened. Assign double amount of homework and quizzes for rest of the week.
    c) Stop class, bring in school psychologist to discuss how everyone is handling the event and "post-traumatic stress disorder."

20. Someone is flashing and tailgating you on the highway, even though you're driving ten over the limit. What do you do?
    a) Move to the right lane
    b) Stay in my lane, it's not safe for this person to drive so fast.
    c) Hit the brakes hard.

21. You see someone littering and it bothers you. What do you do?
    a) Pick up the litter and put it in the trash.
    b) Confront the litterer, explain why littering is bad for society.
    c) Call the police.

22. It's 1976 and you're Bill Gates's secretary. He often loses track of time and is late to his appointments. What do you do to make him on time?
    a) Tell him it's rude to be late and he'll miss his flights.
    b) Tell him the wrong time so he's on time.
    c) Threaten to quit if he can't be on time.

23. Delivery driver arrives to pick up an order you're still preparing. What do you say to him?
    a) It'll be 5 more minutes.
    b) It'll be 5 more minutes, this is a big order.
    c) Hi, how are you?

24. Salesperson calls you and asks "Hi, how are you today?" How do you respond?
    a) I'm fine, thank you. How are you today?
    b) What do you want?
    c) I'm sad. Can you cheer me up?

Answers below, **bold for good fucking manners**, and *italics for good manners*. (Comments are in parenthesis).

1. You're at dinner and want someone to pass you the salt. What do you say?

    a) *Can you please pass the salt, when you get a chance?*

    b) Pass the salt.

    c) Pass me the salt now or I'll hit you.

       (be concise, less is best).

2. You're making a sales call. How do you greet the person you're calling?

    a) This is so and so calling from such and such business. Can I speak to so and so?

    b) *Hi, how are you today?*

    c) *Hi, can I please speak to so and so?*

3. You're a host at a restaurant. How do you greet a customer?

    a) *Hello sir, how are you this lovely evening?*

    b) How many?

    c) *Hi, how are you?*

       (translate what customer is saying and don't waste time).

4. The grocery clerk greets you: "Hi, how are you?" How do you respond?

    a) *I'm fine, thank you. How are you?*

    b) Busy.

    c) None of your business.

       (unless you really are just fine. don't lie, it'll become a habit)

5. Light turns green but the car in front of you doesn't move. What do you do?

    a) Hand on horn until this dipshit moves.

    b) *Don't do anything.*

    c) Tap on the horn.

6. Car behind you honks because the lights green and you're stalled. What do you do?

 a) *Drive and give finger to honker.*

 b) Drive.

 c) *Wait until light turns yellow, then go.*

7. Your daughter loves gymnastics and is about to enter her first meet. She's confident about winning and even thought about the perfect place to hang her blue ribbon. While she did well, she didn't medal, and was devastated. What do you, as a parent, tell her?

 a) *Tell her you thought she was the best.*

 b) *Tell her she has the ability and will surely win next time.*

 c) Tell her she doesn't deserve to win because she didn't work hard enough.

 (be honest, if it turns out you're wrong then you'll be branded a liar).

8. Customer is angry about something. How do you make him less angry?

 a) *Tell him to calm down, everything will be fine.*

 b) Be upset about what the customer is angry about.

 c) *Look concerned and distressed.*

 (treat others as they treat you, mirroring).

9. Your partner tells you you're lazy. How do you respond?

 a) *Takes one to know one, asshole.*

 b) Why am I lazy?

 c) *You never see all the things I do for you.*

 (always acknowledge another person's perspective).

10. Traffic is worse than usual, so you're 15 minutes late to work. What do you say when you show up?

 a) *Sorry I'm late, traffic was awful, I've never seen it this bad.*

b) Sorry I'm late.

c) Sorry I'm late, someone spank me.

(less is best so you don't make excuses).

11. Manager points out the mistake you made. What do you say?

a) Shit, sorry.

b) Sorry, this was the first time I made the mistake.

c) Sorry, but it was really busy.

(less is best so you don't make excuses).

12. You get stopped for speeding. Officer asks you where you're going. How do you respond?

a) It's dark, I can't see the speed limit sign and I'm already late for work!

b) I'm sorry for speeding but I'm late for work and I really can't afford a speeding ticket right now.

c) Work.

(less is best so you don't come off as defensive).

13. Co-worker put something in the wrong place. Manager asks you why it's there. What do you say or do?

a) "She put it there, I didn't do it."

b) Move it to the right place.

c) "I have no idea how it got there."

14. How do you tell employee about a mistake they made?

a) You're a great guy but your calculations here are wrong. Can you fix them, if you don't mind? You're a great team player, btw.

b) These are wrong, fix them.

c) I know this sounds harsh and I don't mean anything personally, but can you look over these calculations again?

(once you make a bullshit sandwich, you'll have to keep adding more bullshit to it to make it palatable).

15. As you're focused on a complicated order, condescending customer tells you that you should smile more if you want a tip. How do you respond?

   a) *"I'm sorry, I'm having a bad day.*

   b) *Smile more.*

   c) **Ask her if she'd like a side order of "Fuck Off" to go with her order.**

   (don't let others bully you).

16. What do you say or do to mother whose daughter is throwing ice cubes at other customers?

   a) *Madam, can you please stop your daughter from throwing ice cubes, if you don't mind.*

   b) Throw ice cubes at them.

   c) **Tell her to get the fuck out.**

   (never state the obvious and avoid arguments, just get rid of them).

17. Customer asks for something that's not on the menu. What's your response?

   a) *No, we don't have that.*

   b) *Restaurant down the street has that, go there.*

   c) **We have something similar, want to try it?**

   (never say "no." If you have to say it, say "fuck off" instead).

18. Your 8-year-old is new at school. He gets shoved out of lunch line and is told to get to the back. He responds by beating the shit out of the kid who bullied him. What's your response?

   a) Ground him and make him apologize to kid he beat up.

   b) **Tell him he did the right thing and to never worry about lawsuits, you'll take care of those if they come up.**

c) *Have your kid apologize to the kid he beat up and have them talk it out. End with hug.*
(show, don't tell)

19. Earthquake during math class! Big enough to topple bookshelves. Nobody is hurt, everyone is okay, just jittery. What do you, as teacher, do?

a) Stop class, act jittery and anxious because that's how you feel.

b) Have students clean up mess and continue class as if nothing happened. Assign double amount of homework and quizzes for rest of the week.

c) *Stop class, bring in school psychologist to discuss how everyone is handling the event and "post-traumatic stress disorder."*

(what famed math instructor Jaime Escalante did)

20. Someone is flashing and tailgating you on the highway, even though you're driving ten over the limit. What do you do?

a) Move to the right lane

b) *Stay in my lane, it's not safe for someone to drive that fast.*

c) *Hit the brakes hard.*

(don't be Karen)

21. You see someone littering and it bothers you. What do you do?

a) Pick up the litter and put it in the trash.

b) *Confront the litterer, explain why littering is bad for society.*

c) *Call the police.*

(show, don't tell, unless you have the power to enforce your request)

22. It's 1976 and you're Bill Gates's secretary. He often loses track of time and is late to his appointments. What do you do to make him on time?

a) *Tell him it's rude to be late and he'll miss his flights.*

b) Tell him the wrong time so he's on time.

25

c) *Threaten to quit if he can't be on time.*

(sometimes lying is okay. In this case, it prevents wasting other people's time).

23. Delivery driver arrives to pick up an order you're still preparing. What do you say to him?

   a) It'll be 5 more minutes.

   b) It'll be 5 more minutes, this is a big order.

   c) Hi, how are you?

   (less is best, never make excuses, and don't waste time)

24. Salesperson calls you and asks "Hi, how are you today?" How do you respond?

   a) I'm fine, thank you. How are you today?

   b) What do you want?

   c) I'm sad. Can you cheer me up?

   (let caller know that your time isn't to be wasted)

Part II
Secondary Principles

When good friends praise a gifted person he often appears to be delighted with them out of politeness and goodwill, but in reality he feels indifferent.

— Friedrich Nietzsche from *Human, All-Too-Human*

Chapter 3
Save Other People Time

If not wasting other people's time is about getting your head out of your ass so you're not a navel gazing lazy piece of shit who is clueless about how your lack of outward attention affects other people, then saving other people time is about being proactive – entering another person's spirit, getting to know them well enough that you can make their lives easier. Even the lazy will appreciate you if you can save them more time so they can waste time doing whatever it is they do. Hedonism takes time too.

Examples include taking someone's shopping cart so they don't have to park it in a designated area because you need a cart, anyway, might as well get it now then later. You're a server and you help a colleague out by picking up some finished plates since you have an extra hand and it's on your way anyway. Neither of the two acts requires you to sacrifice time – your time comes first – but it makes someone else's lives easier and all it takes is being alert to other people's wants and needs.

And even if you do sacrifice a bit of time, like picking up your neighbor's kids because you happen to be in the area, you'll probably get back that time and then some. Point is, people like it when someone is watching out for their best interest because few do. And your ability to save people time is what'll make you successful in life and business.

Wonder how I've been in business for nearly 13 years as I'm writing this, despite being described as "psycho," a "lunatic," and "one of the most difficult personalities in the region"? Because I save people time. When I first opened, I noticed other juice bars closing because their customers complained about the wait time and prices. I decided that that won't happen to me and implemented an ordering system that seems rude to some, but it keeps wait times and prices down. Sure sure, people call me "rude. rude rude," but I've yet to see a review complaining about wait times, and most rave about my prices. It's better to be a prick who saves other people time than a nice person who wastes other people's time. Especially with productive people, you can be as rude as you want to them as long as you save them time because they care more about time and results than feelings. And I care a lot more about making productive people happy than the feelings of some loser with his head up his ass because productive people make life better for me, they save me time. It's okay to be a selfish motherfucker, okay?

Most sales people suck at their jobs because their primary effort is put in being as nice and polite as possible. Nice and polite doesn't sell, there's too much of it around, and the experienced know that it means jack shit or worse. Tits and ass sell, and even then, it still doesn't sell as well as saving other people time because people need time and money to play with tits and ass. So every sales effort should focus on saving a customer's time, not on declaring that you should get business because of how nice and polite you are.

What do you need to do to save other people time? You ask them questions and listen to them. Don't ask too many questions – more than three will often annoy people. But asking people two to three questions will have them like you more because it shows that you're interested in them.

Great inventions save people a lot of time. The airplane has reduced travel time. Imagine how productive Shakespeare could've been if he had a laptop and internet. How many hours of shopping and driving has amazon.com saved people? Those who save people time are remembered. Nice people aren't because, as it'll be shown throughout this book, they waste people's time.

This principle works outside of business relations too. Figure out how to save people time – your parents, intimate partner, strangers – and you'll be rewarded if you don't allow yourself to be used. Ask them questions about what's troubling them. What do they need, what do they want?

The well-mannered are effective, it's the incompetent who are polite, pleading to not be found out.

Chapter 4
Don't Lie

Truth matters, feelings don't, and most lies waste time. So don't lie, that's good fucking manners.

Anglos, especially middle-class Americans, are notorious for lying about stupid shit. "But I'm doing it to make someone feel good, it's for a good cause." Giving your kid a gallon of soda to drink each day might make her feel good too, until she turns diabetic and is a contestant on *The Biggest Loser*. So stop telling grandma – this includes Tina Turner – that she looks just like she did when she was in college. Such compliments, at best, will compel her to reminisce about how she wasted her youth and, at worst, to advertise herself as a $1000 an hour hooker. Lying also invariably violates the principles *Don't waste people's time* and *Save people time*. Not telling someone they fucked up doesn't do the fucker-upper any good because they're not getting honest feedback. One can't improve without honest feedback, okay?

Look around, the reason there are so many losers in America is because, starting in the 1980s, some dipshits decided that people, kids especially, need to be praised all the time instead of criticized for their fuck ups. So they became whiny adults. In response, business schools came up with the Bullshit Sandwich, the management term for "a compliment followed by a criticism followed by a criticism" that good managers are supposed to feed those under them. Alyson Green, writing for slate.com, on the effectiveness of Bullshit Sandwiches (she calls them Crap Sandwiches):

> *Unfortunately, the crap sandwich is fraught with problems. Once your employees recognize what you're doing, they might start bracing for criticism every time you open a conversation with praise. It can also make the praise itself seem insincere...*[8]

31

Green quotes someone on how he/she feels when given a Bullshit Sandwich:

> *I always feel like there's some kind of mild deceit going on, and I'm put off by the feeling that the person didn't respect me enough to just talk to me instead of trying to "handle" me. I really hate feeling like I'm being "handled."*

Sure, the intention is to be tactful, to not be rude. The unintended consequences, however, is a lot of wasted time, for everyone, and mounting tension between manager and employee. Green on the unintended consequences:

> *...it's incredibly common for managers to get so concerned about being tactful that their message gets diluted or missed altogether. Then you're left with a manager who feels frustrated that their feedback didn't work and an employee who didn't get the chance to hear clearly that something needs to change.[9]*

Is the Bullshit Sandwich a lie? It's worse, it's a manipulative and condescending lie. At least the kid who shot his older sister who dressed him up as a girl is lying about who maimed her because he's scared and trying to get out of trouble. What happens when you talk to an adult like he's the kid who shot his sister?

---

[8]https://slate.com/human-interest/2018/08/crap-sandwich-a-sneaky-ill-conceived-managerial-technique-for-giving-negative-feedback.html. *Beware of Bosses Handing Out "Crap Sandwiches"*, by Alison Green Aug. 22, 2018 on slate.com

[9] Ibid.

"Hey Sarah, I've heard you like M and Ms, so I brought some for you. And where did you get that blouse, love the color! Now about your analysis paper..."

That's tactful? That's okay? "But, but but, she really does like M and Ms and I really do like her blouse." And the smarmy guy telling Tits and Ass how beautiful and amazing she is only wants to take photos of her so she can become a supermodel. Give me a fucking break. In any case, even if that's true, it's still a lie to the recipient because the message is confusing. A quote from a manager about how Bullshit Sandwiches distort the message:

> *Even when I think I am being direct, I replay the conversation in my head later and realize I padded the whole thing with "softening" language that only distorts the message. ...*[10]

"Numbers are off here, here, and there, fix 'em" is clear. "You have such good taste in music, could you recommend a new album to me and I love your shoes, where did you get them? And if you don't mind, when you get a chance, to look over the calculations on this chart, something doesn't make sense? I'm heading out for coffee, let me know if I can get you anything" isn't. The recipient likely started to tune out somewhere around the mention of her shoes, and the core message is lost so deep in a mire of bullshit that she has no idea what it is.

Intentions don't matter, results do. Grading people based on their intentions turns them into incompetent and self-righteous assclowns. Imagine if professional athletes were graded on their intentions instead of results, would sports fans continue to watch? "Sorry coach, I didn't mean to fumble the ball, can I get a pat on the back?" How about engineers, you want to hire one graded on his intentions or his track record to build a bridge you're going to use?

---

[10] Ibid.

"But I don't want to come off as rude," says the covert narcissist with an unhealthy aversion to conflict. What's it to you if someone thinks you're rude? If it makes you feel bad about yourself, then you have serious problems that probably begins with an addiction to compliments and a fear of not being liked – put simply, narcissism. Again, well-mannered people are concerned about facts, not feelings. It's not healthy to depend on external validation to feel good about oneself and I believe that we all have an internal moral compass that'll tell us if we've done right or wrong, it's just that they've faded or become corrupted after so many years of schooling and listening to gibberish. Develop that compass by ignoring your ego's need to be liked by all.

This obsession with not being rude has been disastrous for American politics, culture, and society. Like during the Chinese Cultural Revolution, people are afraid to speak their mind about anything. Some who do get canceled (though in truth, most don't, they move on to better positions, this is nothing as bad as the Cultural Revolution). It's given whiners on both sides of politics reasons to not invite dialogue, to instead rant about how offensive something is and storming off after promising to never patronize this or that media outlet or business. Again, American obsession with eradicating rudeness isn't a sign of its civility, it's evidence of narcissism run amok – all who play this game are either obsessed with being liked and/or worshiped. My moral compass tells me to not feed people's egos, to not encourage narcissism, the deadliest of the deadly sins (aka pride, or vanity). If your moral compass tells you the same, then stop it with gratuitous compliments, they're like verbal heroin that fuck people up long run. Well-mannered people may make people cry, but they don't fuck people up. Simon Caldwell, the "mean" British critic from *America's Got Talent*, has been accused of ruining lives for telling the truth. No, he hasn't ruined anyone's lives, it's the accused whose inflated egos are ruining their own lives. The narcissistic ego needs external validation the way a heroin addict needs heroin, they can't go long without it. Healthy egos aren't emotionally affected by external validation or criticism (even if the criticism is gratuitous), they treat them as sometimes useful evaluations to guide their next move. Simon merely helped these whiners recognize the truth about themselves sooner, saving them time. Otherwise, they'd continue to get validation from those with low standards and bad taste and never get anywhere past their basement karaoke station.

Not lying doesn't mean you should always blurt out the truth. If nobody asks you your opinion about something, you probably shouldn't express it. For instance, if a customer I don't know orders something that I think is stupid – orange juice for a cold (all that sugar!) – I'll do as requested without comment. If it's a regular customer I know well, I'll say something: "You can get the same amount of vitamin c without the sugar if you take two bites of bell pepper instead..." That's because this customer and I have built up trust in each other, which means we can and expect to be frank with each other. We can help each other in meaningful ways. Without that trust, keep your mouth shut because less is best.

Chapter 5
Less is Best

Know why every lawyer tells their client to shut the fuck up? Because most people say stupid incriminating shit when they talk without realizing it. Those who are allowed to talk are coached extensively.

Coach yourself similarly. Train yourself to say as little as possible. The more you say, the more likely you'll come off as defensive or whiny; or perhaps gratuitously mean (by either embellishing the truth or adding an unnecessary dig), like a mainstream American journalist covering foreign affairs or national politics. Give "yes" and "no" answers, don't explain yourself unless asked to do so. Don't ramble on about anything, especially about yourself, unless invited to do so, because few, if any, care about most of what's going on in your head and your life. Ask questions instead. No, not "do you like me?" or "what do you think of my outfit?" type questions narcissists ask. Questions about the world, like "why did Russia invade Ukraine?" "Why does it rain so much?" Or questions about the person you're talking to: "Why do you wear shoes?" "What's the color of your underwear?" Aim to ask questions people don't hear often. And *listen* to their response, don't assume you know how the conversation will go, making a wrong assumption makes you look like a dull and self-involved dolt. A question like "how are you?" is fine, even if hackneyed, if you're sincere, you don't assume you know how someone will answer, and you listen intently for the response. Tuning out is bad manners, okay?

Less is best will help you pay attention to other people instead of the sound of your own voice. Starting to understand the main theme of this book? It's similar to Robert Greene's *Art of Seduction* – get rid of YOUR narcissistic tendencies in order to have good fucking manners and, nod to Greene, to become more seductive. Having good fucking manners is about becoming more seductive by being less narcissistic and more authentic (say only what you believe is true or don't say anything at all).

Be Concise

Unlike a pared down language that's grammatically and lexically simple like Chinese, English allows for a lot of wordiness and thus, pomposity. (English also allows for more precision, which has its advantages in matters of science and philosophy). There's no word for "quite" or "rather" in Chinese, someone is simply "stupid," never "quite stupid." Or that stinky tofu "tastes good," not "tastes rather good." Americans aren't the worst offenders, they're less likely to use meaningless or obfuscating words than Brits are, but they still do it too much. Too many adverbs for instance. Here's how a narcissist in love with her own voice speaks and writes:

> *The amazing author profoundly utilizes many symbols to creatively symbolize his very meaningful ideas.*

Which sounds fucktarded, even if many are impressed with it for its extraneous syllables. It doesn't get to the point and muddles the situation it's describing - this is usually deliberate, it's a misguided attempt to sound more intellectual, which we'll discuss in the next chapter. How would you edit such a wordy sentence? How about this:

> *The author uses symbols to illustrate his ideas.*

Does this edit make you feel less at loss about the CONTENT and MEANING of what she's trying to say? Does it get right to the point? Don't waste people's time to make yourself look good, because someone will notice that you look like someone with good manners – a pretentious fucktard – than someone with good fucking manners. Focus on communicating substance, not style.

Avoid Passive Voice

The passive voice is wordier and sounds less trustworthy than the active voice. It also makes the speaker come off as timid and irresponsible.

Monzo.com is an online bank that makes an effort to clarify their terms and conditions for their customers. Instead of saying, "a refund will be given to you" (passive voice, nine syllables), they say "we'll give you a refund" (active voice, six syllables) as part of their tone guidelines. The passive voice tries to shift responsibility from the party in question by putting distance between themselves and the action. "Sure, you'll receive a refund, but not necessarily because we fucked up. In fact, you probabl fucked up but to keep your business, we'll give you a refund anyway." The active voice, in contrast, takes responsibility for whatever may happen (e.g., misunderstanding) to you, the customer by identifying wh will give you the refund.

Part V of this book – Exercises – provides more examples so you can practice communicating actively and responsibly instead of passively and timidly.

Less is Best Makes You Sound More Powerful

You'll be treated with more respect. For example, CEOs say less than most people (despite being asked more questions than most, I assume). From slab.com blog post titled "We Analyzed How 38 CEOs Send Emails—Here's What We Found."

> *CEOs are notorious for sending brief, standardized responses to emails and know exactly how to get their point across as quickly and succinctly as possible. Jeff Bezos and Elon Musk are the mos extreme, and maybe the best, examples of this.*

Jeff Bezos often responds with "?". Elon Musk uses "WTF?"

Robert Greene's 4th law of power is "Always say less than necessary."[11] Reason:

> *The less you say, the more intimidating and powerful you are.*
> *Always say less than necessary.*

Here's where this etiquette book differs from his advice. He recommends being "vague and ambiguous, leaving the meaning to others to interpret." That works if you're powerful like Jeff Bezos and Elon Musk. For the rest of us, focus on clarity. I agree that there are times you should be mysterious – romantic relationships, for instance – innuendo and undertone can make you seem more interesting and thus, attractive. But in most situations, most people aren't in a position to use mystery to advance anyone's interest, it'll just annoy people and they'll ignore you. Where Greene and I agree is that" saying little avoids the risk of saying something foolish, which can be costly."

How foolish?

People say stupid shit all the time. "Oh, come on, it's not that cold, I've been in much colder climates," replies the narcissist who must make every conversation about how awesome he is. "Don't be nervous," says the well-meaning to the tense competitor. Will telling someone to stop feeling what she's feeling make her less skittish? Or will it make jumpy Jimmy even more anxious? Or are those words meant to make the speaker feel better about himself because he thinks he's making a situation better? How do you like it when someone tells you to not be angry, or sad, or neurotic, whatever it is you're feeling? Does it make you feel guilty about your feelings, like you have no right to feel that way? Does it make you feel worse? Again, intentions don't matter – narcissists are in love with

---

[11] *The 48 Laws of Power (1998)*

intentions and "well-meaning people are sometimes the most dangerous"[12] – results do. Stick to acknowledging that you're listening to the other person, that's what people want to hear.

Less Because You're Boring as a Faucet Drip

Or at least more boring than you think you are, especially if you don't think narcissism is your Original Sin.

People don't care about most of what's going on in your head. Do you really need to post something about it finally raining? Or that you turned on the heat in your house for the first time this unusually warm season? Do you care about what most people are thinking and saying? Say enough of what's irrelevant to people and they'll tune you out. Say only what matters to people and they'll soon listen intently to you, especially those who hate what you say.

And don't try to be funny. In fact, you'll be funnier by keeping quiet instead of telling a lame joke like "don't spend all of that at the strip club, haha." You'll also be funnier if you don't lie and describe what you see, think, and feel as precisely as possible. Isn't that what successful stand-up comedians do, they blurt out what everyone's thinking but are afraid to say? Sure, you'll piss off a lot of people but the goal here isn't to be inoffensive – petty, innocuous, and unoriginal – it's to express yourself with good fucking manners so people will take you seriously instead of as one would a Trader Joe's cashier.

---

[12] *Once Upon a Road Trip* by Angela N. Blount (2013)

Chapter 6
Show, Don't Tell

A customer told me that, after he moved to Seattle, he posted an online dating profile. All he wrote was "Hey, I'm David." He posted a dozen photos of himself doing stuff like a cannonball dive, surfing, ziplining, bridge jumping, etc. He's good looking, but nothing special, and he's not chiseled. Yet his verbally minimalist profile probably did better than 99.8% of profiles, he immediately got around a dozen legitimate inquiries from women – that's rare, usually men must reach out to women to get a response.

By showing, instead of telling about himself, he provides more evidence of his income, hobbies, health status, and sense of adventure than he ever can with words. Saying so little also makes him mysterious and thus, more attractive. Tits and Ass is thinking: "wonder what he does for a living so that he has enough free time and can afford to do all these cool activities?"

Sure, most of the women this profile attracted probably aren't marriage material, and that's not what he was looking for. He was new in town and wanted someone cute and fun to show him around, that's all. And that's what he got because showing is more effective than telling.

So spend less time telling people who you think you are: "I'm funny," "I'm hard-working," I'm loyal." Those who haven't accomplished much shouldn't say anything about who they think they are. In fact, we should send every teenager who mentions her "awesome communication skills" on her resume to an arctic labor camp. Have them harvest timber, then we'll see how well their mastery of gossip girl speak serves them outside their world of vapid people trying to appear virtuous. Falling trees are a lot more dangerous than any smear campaign, perhaps they'll learn to communicate well when the consequences of not doing so is death by splat.

By telling people who you think you are, you're showing your standards. That leaves you vulnerable because people are judged less by their accomplishments, and more by their standards. Put it this way: is it better to finish last in the Olympics, or first in the pee-wee league? Would you prefer to hang out with the person who brags about winning the pee-wee league, or the Olympian who makes self-effacing jokes about finishing last? If Tasby thinks he's smart because he graduated with a Sociology degree from Sonoma State University, there's someone with a degree in Physics from Princeton who thinks he has low standards, even if she's too kind to admit it.

Whether you show or tell, people will assess you based on THEIR standards, not yours. Bravado won't fool those with higher standards than yours for long. Those with good manners don't understand that because they're distracted by their need to be liked and admired, so they label those with higher standards as "rude" and only hang out with those with comparable or lower standards. That's why Chubby Cheryl prefers to hang out with Fat Frannie than Skinny Stacey, she feels sexier that way. Those with good fucking manners hang out with those who can make them better, the ones with comparable and higher standards than theirs. They don't mind feeling inferior, because that's their first step toward improvement and mastery. We learn from those more accomplished than us, not just in career, but also in personal relationships or whatever else matters to you. You define your success.

People Love Stories

If you're going to tell, tell stories that SHOW how people are. Instead of merely describing yourself, tell people stories to SHOW how you were an imbecile, or courageous, or are funny, and so forth. Telling a story about

42

how you survived an encounter with a black bear is a lot more interesting and less abstract than saying "I'm courageous." To begin with, stories provide evidence of who you are as a person. Second, it allows the person you're communicating with to experience your life, which is how people bond. And finally, it'll make you less self-absorbed and more aware of different perspectives of who you are, because someone may interpret your experiences differently from you, the feedback is invaluable. Unless you're Woke and believe that you, and only you, have the right to define who you are as a person and everyone else should confirm your identity. In which case, carry on living your miserable, tyrannical, and ensconced life.

Telling engrossing stories isn't easy, so work on it. Write about any happening that interests you, your thoughts on paper is a mirror of yourself. Read fiction, doesn't matter if it's considered good or bad by others. Just note which storytelling mechanisms resonate you. Then emulate, and gradually, you'll find your own story telling voice so that you can effectively tell to show.

When to Tell Someone to Do Something

Tell someone to do something only when you think they will or when you have the power to enforce your request. You lose respect and power when someone you've asked to do something doesn't. Watch parents pleading – "please this, please that" -- with their kids to do this and that but they rarely do because they've learned that there aren't any consequences when they don't do as asked. This is true of dogs too, some trainers insist that you force your dog to sit the first time you ask, otherwise they think it's optional. The more your requests are ignored, the more powerless you'll feel and become. And only say "please" if you're in a position of power in relation to the person you're talking to and you want to relax the power dynamic so they can be frank and at ease with you: a "please, have a seat," for example. Otherwise, "please" sounds like begging and it implies the option to not do as you ask. The grocery store sign should read "return carts," not "please return carts."

Chapter 7
Treat Others as They Treat You

Not everyone wants to be treated the way you want to be treated, the world doesn't revolve around you. Just because Sentimental Sally doesn't like getting yelled at when she fucks up doesn't mean the NFL player who fumbles the ball doesn't want to get chewed out by the coach. Those who are responsible and conscientious want to be berated after fucking up because it makes them feel better, they like being held responsible for their fuck ups. It's the irresponsible – they have inflated and therefore sensitive egos – who hate getting yelled at because they never feel like it's their fault.

People have different tastes, desires, and needs. Just because you like cilantro doesn't mean everyone else likes it. Just because Dipshit Doug Evans enjoys inserting gerbils up his ass doesn't mean you want to do the same. Just because most Americans are brainwashed into thinking that everyone desires Western style democracy doesn't mean most people in the world want it. Think of all the bad sex that happens when people treat others the way they want to be treated. Does everyone want to be tied up and have their ass slapped red? Probably not for those who get off on doing the slapping.

Treating others as you want to be treated, then, is the quintessential narcissistic life philosophy. These are the people who project their needs, wants, and desires onto other people. They say rude shit like:

- "How can you NOT like [this or that] (implying that those who don't like what he likes have bad taste).
- "If I were you" (even though that person is anything but you AND this is how narcissists shift attention back to themselves when talking about someone else's problems).

45

Narcissists think everyone wants what they want and get offended when someone doesn't. That's why they're condescending, especially when they try to be polite. Examples of patronizing "polite" phrases dipshits use to make themselves look and feel superior:

- "Relax..."
- "I actually like that idea..."
- "I hear you, but..."

That's what you get when you mix narcissism with good intentions: passive aggressive, genteel bullying.

Some are thinking: why not treat others the way they want to be treated, wouldn't that be nicer? It would, but you risk living as a doormat. Do you really want to be friends with someone who takes advantage of you by never reciprocating because she has a princess complex? Or are you going to be a hermit to avoid such people, who'll look for you to take advantage of you? The purpose of good fucking manners is to get the dipshits out of your life so you can live better. And in any case, most people are too self-absorbed to figure out how others want to be treated, most project their own wants, needs, and fears onto everyone else instead of recognizing uniqueness (yes, uniqueness even though individuals are rarely as unique as they think they are). That's why the bookkeeper who hates working more than 40 hours a week during tax season will never marry her crush, the CPA who works 80 a week, because she wrongly assumes that he hates work as much as she does and works solely to feed a greed for money. She wants to change him for the "better," – to be more like her – even though she's the one with the problem: laziness rooted in a dismal attitude about the purpose of life (avoid pain at all costs). How many people who work for vacation and retirement wonder why a billionaire would keep working so much, why not retire and party like it's 1999? Or why NFL Tom Brady would keep playing into his mid-forties, why not play with his kids and bang his hot (ex) wife now that he's the GOAT and worth a quarter of a billion? Most, because they can't imagine anyone with a different vision and approach to life than their own.

Ironically, if you really want to treat others as they want to be treated, you should treat them the way they treat you. That is, mimic/mirror them, as psychologists put it. Here's the definition of mirroring that I like and found on brides.com.

> *Mirroring is a subconscious occurrence that can create a feeling of comfort because humans are evolutionarily designed to be attracted to people who are similar to them. When employed consciously, it plays a huge role in getting to know someone and establishing a level of comfort together.*

Bill Gates was known as a mean motherfucker when he was building Microsoft. His favorite phrase was "this is the stupidest..." How should you deal with him when he screams that your idea is "the stupidest I've ever heard"? Pick:

a. Tell him he's right and that you'll work on it more.
b. Cry and tell him that he's hurting your feelings.
c. Ask him if he's done and continue with your presentation.

In every biography I've read, the correct answer is C, throw it back at him, which is what Bill Gates would do. Picking C tells Bill Gates that you're an extension of himself, you've anticipated his reactions and you're not afraid of him. Mirroring works because we are narcissists, we love the reflection of ourselves, even if we find it ugly. That's why fat people tend to hang out with fat people and shun those who try to slimdown. That's why people hang out in echo chambers and seek the familiar.

So Princess Cuntface will probably like you more if you use her the way she uses you, and definitely if she sees you using someone else the same way she does. Sure, she won't like being used, but she loves watching the reflection of herself in someone else. Meanwhile, nice people finish last because they suck at theater, they're too self-absorbed to figure out how to play different parts of an act, they can't figure out what others are thinking and feeling. That's why they resort to a default nice act that gets boring fast. So practice mirroring the way a good actress practices her craft. Practice empathy, not sympathy, figure out what people are thinking and feeling. Those with "good manners" confuse sympathy for empathy, they mix-up feeling bad for someone for empathy when it's actually narcissistic projection ("if I were her, I'd..."). Those with good fucking manners know the difference between the two and are thus able to enter the spirit of another.

But I don't want to be Princess Cuntface

You're probably more of one than you think. In any case, that's fine, then say no to her and move on if playing villain isn't part of your repertoire. The goal of good fucking manners isn't to be liked by everyone, it's to attract those who'll help you to live the life you want to live. Having good fucking manners means fewer but better friends and you'll be better at helping people. Question:

> Customer walks in and is pissed about the haircut one of your colleagues gave to his daughter, her schoolmates say she looks like a muppet. How should you respond? Be:
>
> a) Apologetic
> b) Sad
> c) Angry

Correct answer is C, be angry, not at him but on his behalf. Choices A and B will make the customer angrier because nobody is acknowledging his anger. People don't want sympathy – someone feeling sorry for them – they want empathy, someone who acknowledges how they're feeling and thinking. Yet customer service keeps choosing A or B, despite adverse consequences: usually the customer getting angrier. People, and this paradoxically includes Woke Zombies who've made victimhood fashionable, don't like to be pitied because it makes them look pathetic. People, on the other hand, connect well with those who mimic (not mock) them because that's empathy, that's entering the spirit of the other person to feel what he perceives, think what she thinks. That's why people hate it when they hear rude comments like these:

- Don't be sad (when you are)
- But you're so beautiful (when you feel ugly)
- Don't be nervous (when you are)
- Don't be angry at me (even though this person just did something shitty to you and won't take responsibility for it)
- That wasn't my intention (even though intentions are irrelevant)

In none of the cases above is the talker empathizing, he's either pitying (which makes him feel better about himself) or acting defensively. Yet how did we get to the point where saying shit like that is normal and acceptable, encouraged even? Are the intentions even honorable? Is this why so many people feel lonely, even in their echo chambers?

Another example: I own a couple of restaurants and one of our delivery services is Doordash. Doordash has its customer service reps read off a script for common situations. This script teaches them to be "polite." That is, use many words to say how much they care about your situation and how hard they'll work to fix the problem. That's a mistake, as anyone who has worked in the restaurant industry knows. The customer service rep doesn't see what's going on the other end, and that other side might

49

be experiencing a backup of orders. Meanwhile, the customer service rep is yapping useless words, taking up valuable time. What Doordash shoul teach their customer service reps is to mirror the customer (in this case, the merchant experiencing problems with the system). If the customer sounds relaxed and is chatty, be like that, if time allows. If a customer is impatient, get to the point and solve the problem in as few words as possible. Wasting people's time is what happens when you practice good manners. With good fucking manners, you'll fix problems efficiently and people will need you for your competence instead of tolerating you for being nice.

What should one say instead of "don't be sad"? We'll explore in *Part III Situations.*

Part III
Situations

Half of the harm that is done in this world
Is due to people who want to feel important.

-- TS. Eliot (*The Cocktail Party,* 1949)

Chapter 8
Phone Etiquette

Most people – salespeople included – have atrocious phone manners. Two common caller introduction mistakes:

- Hi, is so-and-so there?
- Hi, how are you?

What's the first thing people want to know when they get a phone call? Who the caller is. Yet most people don't identify themselves when they cold-call someone. What makes people think they deserve access to someone they don't know? Narcissism, that's what. These callers only care about what they want, and not what the person they're calling wants. These people suck at sales and negotiation.

"Hi, how are you?" violates the Don't Waste Time principle. It's often not a question, it's meant to announce that one has good manners and therefore deserves attention and reward. But I haven't noticed a correlation between polite behavior and good character. In fact, I've noticed that polite people usually turn out to be either incompetent and/or wretched and despicable. At least one study has reached a similar conclusion.

The Annual Meeting of the Association for Computational Linguistics (AMACL) in Beijing just released their study's result that those who are "excessively polite" are considerably more likely to betray peers or comrades than those who are not very polite. In short, overly polite people are likely to be the most

---

[13] https://en.brilio.net/personality/science-says-overly-polite-people-are-dangerous-and-this-is-why-1604042.html

potential backstabbers in your social sphere.[13]

Why then do so many Americans correlate "good manners" with good character and why are they easily impressed with virtue signaling? Unfortunately, we can't ask serial killer Ted Bundy – so nice that he worked for a suicide prevention line -- why Americans are the most gullible and uncritical demographic in the history of the world because he's dead.[14]

How to Respond to Rude Introductions

One option is honesty. Like this:

> *"Is so-and-so there?"*
> *"Yes, she is."*
> *"Can I speak with her?"*
> *"No."*

It's also fun to fuck with the caller (fucking with someone isn't lying, it's playing a prank). Like this:

> *"Is so-and-so there?"*
> *"No"*
> *"When is the best time to reach her?"*
> *"4am weekends"*

Another option is to hang up on them. I do this when I'm busy.

> *"Is so-and-so there?"*

---

[14] "He was a very nice person," Bundy's friend Marlin Lee Vortman, whom he met through his work as a Republican activist, says in the 2019 Netflix documentary,
Conversations with a Killer: The Ted Bundy Tapes.
"He was the kind of guy you'd want your sister to marry."

"No" [hang up]

If you're curious about the caller, try this:

"Is so-and-so there?"
"Who is calling?"
"I'm so-and-so from so-and-so."

Correct Introductions

Examples:

- "I'm calling from Dr. Hwang's office, can I talk to so-and-so?"
- "I'm Siobhan, from Comcast. I want to help you save money."
- "This is Velma, from Spanish class. Is this Daphne?
- "I'm calling from Medical Sales Company, who can I talk to the owner about equipment upgrades?

Always announce yourself, either who you are or which group you represent. Then announce your intention in as few words as possible.

Picking Up Calls

The most common mistake is not identifying yourself or the group you represent to the caller. Identifying who you are or the business you represent lets the caller know if she called the right number, the first order of business of most calls. Now that we have cell phones that identify friends and family who are calling, the identification step can be skipped between those familiar with each other.

- "Jeromin residence."
- "Alive Juice Bar, place your order."
- "Grocery Outlet, how can I help you?"

- "Eve speaking"
- "Alex here, who's calling?"

If you don't want to identify yourself, say this:

- Who's calling?

Just don't pick up the phone and say "hello." It's unnecessary, it just adds another meaningless line to the conversation.

Taking messages

Repeat the message – phone numbers especially -- to the sender. Most communication is miscommunication, so double check your work. Never assume that your listening and comprehension skills are perfect. Double checking your work is good fucking manners.

Chapter 9
The Art of Being Mean

It's okay to be mean, really. Even Jesus Christ was a mean motherfucker when people fucked with his shit, flipping tables and all. From the book of Matthew 21:12-13:

> And Jesus entered the temple[a] and drove out all who sold and bought in the temple, and he overturned the tables of the money changers and the seats of those who sold pigeons. (13) He said to them, "It is written, 'My house shall be called a house of prayer,' but you make it a den of robbers."

That's right, anyone who thinks Jesus was a nice dude probably thinks Pedro the priest doesn't jerk off to biddibongbiddibing.

It's human nature to be mean, though some are naturally meaner than others. Those are details best left for another treatment, let's start with the premise that there are good and bad ways to be mean. You can be mean in a way that's bad for your mental health, for instance. Which implies that there are ways to be mean that's healthy for you. You can also be gratuitously mean. You may not be mean enough, or at least not mean in an effective way. And you can be mean in a way that'll attract those who can make your life better and drive away those who'll make you miserable. In summary, the art of being mean is worth thinking about. So let's examine how most people are mean in Anglo cultures (e.g. US, UK, Canada) since I'm primarily writing for the Anglo audience.

Sarcasm

Anglo cultures (e.g. US, UK, Canada) love sarcasm. It's everywhere and most are proud to be sarcastic. Here's the dictionary definition of sarcasm:

> *the use of irony to mock or convey contempt.*

Here's the Wiki definition:

> *a sharp, bitter, or cutting expression or remark; a bitter gibe or taunt*

Here's the Greek etymology of sarcasm:

> *Greek sarkasmos "sarcasm," from sarkazein "to tear flesh, bite the lips in rage, sneer,"*

Which means most Americans, without realizing it, are bitter people who prefer to express contempt in a joking manner so as to not take ownership for feeling and expressing it. And people wonder why middle-class America is the most medicated demographic in the world. When people dress feelings they're uncomfortable with — hate and anger — as "harmless, sassy wit," they become emotionally corrupt. One can't be nice AND sarcastic, just as one can't be a nice rapist. Pick one or the other, one can't have it both ways. Trying to have it both ways is how batshit crazy begins.

And just how mean does one need to be? Usually not mean enough to warrant using sarcasm to express what's bothering you, the razor blades sarcasm brings to most fights are gratuitous and excessive. Check out this opening line from an Emily Warren music video:

> *Good news Riley, looks like you're going to be working the entire weekend*

That's a typical sarcastic remark Americans make. How is that funny? It isn't funny to Riley, who was looking forward to having the weekend off. Maybe it's funny to those who really really hate Riley and wish the worst for her? Is the speaker marveling at his own so-called wit, at Riley's expense? Wouldn't it be kinder if he'd said this instead:

> *Riley, I'm sorry. I know you were looking forward to taking this weekend off, but we really need you to work this weekend. I'll make it up to you.*

Point is, a lot of people make sarcastic remarks when it's inappropriate to do so. This creates negativity that's somehow packaged as funny to those who delight in other people's follies and misfortunes.

If the intention is to be bitter and mean, then fine, continue with the sarcasm. But don't tell everyone how nice you are because that's about as honest as American foreign policy. Save the sarcasm for when you're really really pissed, like ready to choke that person out and pee on him pissed. Here's how Jesus used sarcasm to taunt a mob that wanted to stone him:

> They picked up stones again to stone Him. Jesus answered them, "I showed you many good works from the Father; for which of them are you stoning Me?" – John 10:31–32

Ouch. Here's another example of sarcasm used appropriately, someone asked Moses if he was fucking up after he led his wandering Jews out of Egypt:

> Was there a lack of graves in Egypt, that you took us away to die in the wilderness?" Exodus 14:11

58

Another example from Hamlet Act 1, Scene 2, in which Hamlet gets pissed about his mom marrying his uncle way too soon after his father has died:

> "Thrift, thrift, Horatio! The funeral bak'd meats did coldly furnish forth the marriage tables."

In the above three examples, sarcasm is used only in dire situations and its purpose isn't to joke around, it's to elucidate what's really happening. To use sarcasm to joke about everyday situations is to use it inappropriately, with disastrous consequences.

There's nothing wrong with feeling contempt and taunting another person. Even Jesus felt contempt toward the Pharisees and had sharp words for them. It's the dishonesty about one's intentions and sense of self that's toxic and bad for mental health. If you're going to be mean, be unabashedly mean and take responsibility for it instead of dressing it up as a joke. This is how Tucker Max, New York Times bestselling author of *I Hope They Serve Beer in Hell* and *Assholes Finish First*, introduces himself:

> *My name is Tucker Max, and I am an asshole.*

Which he is, read his books if you don't believe me. But at least he's not emotionally corrupt and batshit crazy because he's *honest* about his meanness. And his meanness has a point – he's calling out posers, self-righteous dipshits, really. His meanness is a gratifying counterpoint to the humorless, passive-aggressive narratives that losers chirp around to virtue signal their moral superiority when in fact, they are cruel, vile, and incompetent. Tucker Max is mean and he makes the world a better place.

"Dangerous Faggot" Milo Yiannapoulos also lauds the virtues of being mean, to be a "virtuous troll" as he calls it. For him, the game of political and moral discourse is no different from a game of football – to not be mean is to forfeit the game. One must speak with teeth instead of being muzzled by political correctness. That's because:

> The progressive Left is dedicated to the annihilation of America and every surviving libertarian and conservative person in it. The Left's gratuitous vandalism of American institutions and its hostility to the principles that have made this country great cannot be fought with essays in magazines. The Left can only win by forcing us onto the uneven playing field of political correctness. I choose war.

Play the fucking game right – land your punches -- or go home, okay? That means avoiding euphemisms and describing what you see with succinct precision.

How to Mean the Correct Way

First, take responsibility for being mean, what's the point of hiding that you're a mean person? In other words, be honest and authentic. When you announce your intention to be mean instead of hiding it in a pile of fake good intentions and lame jokes, you'll feel better about yourself, and your meanness might make the world a better place. Do you want to live intentionally or not? Because if you're not living intentionally, you'll have no idea when you're being mean. You'll be mean *while* you think you're the nicest person in the whole wide world, perhaps because your job title or degree (BA in Social Justice!) says so. That's the most treacherous type of meanness because it's driven by hubris and detachment from social reality.

Paul Graham, the billionaire co-founder of the start-up accelerator, Y-Combinator, once tweeted, "The most surprising thing I've learned from being involved with nonprofits is that they are a magnet for sociopaths.

One's naive reaction is "Why would nonprofits attract them? Nonprofits do good!" But the defining quality of nonprofits is to make no profit, not to do good." Those with good manners virtue signal, those with good fucking manners get shit done.

Euphemisms

Mean people avoid them. They're a waste of time, dangerous lies really. But Anglos love them because they think it makes them high sounding, as if their shit don't stink. Example: in Chinese, the restroom is "stinky place." In Anglo nations, the "stinky place" is the "restroom," reality scrubbed clean. Think about that.

Other examples: secretary has morphed to "administrative assistant" to "project coordinator." Janitors became "custodians" and now "custodial engineers." You think the title change confers upon them more respect or does the pretentiousness of it all make them look pathetic, even though I doubt many of them requested the title changes. Then there's self-aggrandizement, where people start some bullshit business, no employees or office, and call themselves a "CEO." In the American socio-cultural world, Black people went from "nigger" to "negro" to "African American" in less than 100 years with nothing to show for it, unemployment rate for Blacks has consistently been double the rate for Whites since they started to keep track of that data in 1950, regardless of who is in office. What are fat people called now and has it improved obesity rates? How about those pronouns, are they a source of freedom or dysfunction? And people wonder why so many Americans suffer from identity crisis and are thus the most medicated demographic in history. This is what happens when good manners are based on equal respect for all.

Still don't think euphemisms are dangerous lies? How about "quantitative easing" for "printing a shitload of money to fund stupid shit, including wars"? "Friendly fire" for "deadly accidents in the name of war." "Collateral damage" when a bomb misses and takes out a village of civilians. A friend of mine who works for a major weapons manufacture is required to call the bombs he designs "ordnances."

The flip side of softening the blow of reality is to exaggerate the trials and tribulations of those you don't like. In the West, the Tiananmen Square Protests of 1989 became the "Tiananmen Square Massacre," blending elements of truth – deadly city-wide riots and a large student protest – to create a helluva story since discredited by WikiLeaks[15] and Western journalists such as Gregory Clark.[16] Russian invasion of Ukraine as "unprovoked," even though Pat Buchanan and University of Chicago political scientist John Mearsheimer have warned about the potential consequences of US aggression toward Russia since the late 1990s. The moral certitude and self-righteousness of the Anglo mainstream is breathtaking. George Orwell on the source of this madness:

> Our language becomes ugly and inaccurate because our thoughts are foolish, but the slovenliness of our language makes it easier for us to have foolish thoughts.[17]

Put simply, euphemisms make people stupid. So stop using them if you want to have good fucking manners, it's better to be mean than stupid. Dipshits will call you mean, which you're proud to say you are. George Orwell, one more time:

---

[15] Link to Wikileaks regarding Tiananmen Square is broken (interesting). So, tr https://www.telegraph.co.uk/news/worldnews/wikileaks/8555142/Wikileaks-no-bloodshed-inside-Tiananmen-Square-cables-claim.html

[16] https://www.japantimes.co.jp/opinion/2008/07/21/commentary/birth-of-a massacre-myth/

[17] https://saharareporters.com/2010/11/25/george-orwell-%E2%80%93-politic and-english-language#:~:text=The%20decline%20of%20a%20language,us%20to%20have%20f oolish%20thoughts.

The great enemy of clear language is insincerity. When there is a gap between one's real and one's desired aims, one turns as it were instinctively to long words and exhausted idioms.

Be mean by being honest, transparent, and concise. And save the sarcasm for when you're justifiably and thoroughly pissed off.

The Customer is Wrong

For details of how to cruel to someone, buy the upcoming book, *The Customer is Wrong,* release date January 2024. There you'll see how to get inside the heads of those you don't like and fuck them up.

Chapter 10
Be Kind, Not Nice

It's not healthy to be nice. From Psyche Central, on Type C personality:

> In recent years, a cluster of personality characteristics has come to
> be identified as the Type C personality, someone who is at
> heightened risk for a slew of afflictions, from colds to asthma
> to cancer. In contrast with the Type A person (who angers easily
> and has difficulty keeping feelings under wraps) and the Type B
> person (who has a healthier balance of emotional expressiveness),
> the Type C person is a suppressor, a stoic, a denier of feelings. He
> or she has a calm, outwardly rational, and unemotional
> demeanor, but also a tendency to conform to the wishes of
> others, a lack of assertiveness, and an inclination toward feelings
> of helplessness or hopelessness.[18]

Examples: she hates football but pretends to like it to attract more men.
He doesn't want to work the holidays but always agrees to do so with an
insincere smile. She hates her haircut but won't tell the hairdresser he
fucked up because she doesn't want to risk hurting his feelings. He
doesn't like his food but won't complain about it until he gets home and
unleashes his anger anonymously on yelp. She won't call her husband the
lazy piece of shit he is because she's conflict adverse. There's a lot of quiet
stewing going on here.

The above cited description of Type C can be more nuanced. It's not
that Type C denies feelings (and thoughts), they deny *specific feelings and
thoughts,* which in the American socio-cultural context typically means
anger and hate, murder and mutilation.

---

[18] No longer on the Internet.

Canadian physician Gabor Mate...began to notice a pattern: individuals who were unable to express anger, who didn't seem to recognize the primacy of their own needs, and who were constantly doing for others, appeared to be the ones most susceptible to a slew of ailments, from asthma, rheumatoid arthritis, and lupus to multiple sclerosis and amyotrophic lateral sclerosis. These conditions are all autoimmune disorders. Mate claims that, when an individual engages in a long-term practice of ignoring or suppressing legitimate feelings–when he or she is just plain too nice–the immune system can become compromised and confused, learning to attack the self rather than defend it.[19]

Again, we need more nuance, as above description makes it seem as if nice people are martyrs. They're not, some of them are raging narcissists who write purple prose, Albert Camus reminds us in *The Fall* (aka "Confessions of a Nice Guy"). That tension, that dissonance between the inner narcissist and the outer martyr means there's going to be a lot of ice cream and chocolate to medicate depression. Which is why some personality type researchers have noticed that Type C personality "is [more likely to be] a consumer of a diet high in sugar, high in saturated/trans-fats, and high in processed and refined foods."[20] They're emotional eaters because they're emotionally corrupt. More of Mate's observations:

Emotional expression, in Mate's view is, absolutely essential because feelings serve to alert the individual to what is dangerous or unwholesome–or, conversely, to what is helpful and nourishing–so that the person can either take protective action against the thread or move toward the beneficial stimulus. If someone never gets angry, this reflects an unhealthy inability or

[19] https://stevemehta.com/type-c-personality-emotionally-repressed/
[20] Pg. 110, from *Take Control: A Guide to Holistic Living* By Linda Mundorff. iUniverse Inc. (2006)

unwillingness to *defend personal integrity.* Such "boundary confusion" can ultimately become a matter of life and death. If someone just cannot say no, Mate argues, his or her body will end up saying it in the form of illness or disease. [21]

Put simply, nice people are fuck ups because they're emotionally corrupt.

Nicest Girl in the Whole World

I once dated someone known as the "nicest girl in the whole world." She always smiled, was always "pleasant," said her "thank yous" and prefaced every request with "please." A month into our relationship and I found her lazy, petty, fragile, and insecure. She was a narcissist addicted to flattery. Her eyes would light up like a teenage boy seeing titties for the first time every time she'd receive a compliment. She'd fish for them online. She demanded that I give her frequent compliments because she was insecure and failing to reach her life goals, she didn't have the confidence to maintain a stable ego on her own. She lacked that confidence because she wasn't living up to her narcissistic delusions about herself – deep down, we know who we really are and what we deserve.

Point is, don't mistake nice for good character. Nice people are nice not because they're good people, but either because they want to be liked (a mild narcissist) or because they need to be admired (a narcissist), worshipped even (a raging narcissist). There may be a few nice types who are truly kind and sincere too. My experience has been that nice is a façade meant to hide either wickedness or incompetence, often both.

Here are some examples of nice people acting like self-absorbed dipshits, from Chapter 7 of this book, they say stupid shit like:

☐   Don't be sad (when you are)

---

[21] https://stevemehta.com/type-c-personality-emotionally-repressed/

- ☐ But you're so beautiful (when you feel ugly, not when you're fishing for compliment)
- ☐ Don't be nervous (when you are)
- ☐ Don't be angry at me (even though this person just did something shitty to you and won't take responsibility for it)
- ☐ That wasn't my intention (even though intentions are irrelevant)

The alternative to nice is to be kind. That is, acknowledge another person's feelings and thoughts as legitimate, even if you don't agree with them. Joust don't dismiss them. If you do that, you'll be more likely to replace above comments with:

- Why are you sad?
- What about you is making you feel ugly?
- It's normal to be nervous.
- Why are you angry at me?
- How can we fix the problem, how can I make it up to you?

In four of the five above, a conversation is started that's focused on the other person. People with good fucking manners aren't self-absorbed so they try to enter another person's spirit so they can perceive and feel as another does.

In other words, it doesn't matter if you think the person who feels ugly is beautiful. You may have different eyes, taste, or standards. What's important is to understand why that person feels ugly and perhaps work with the person to fix the problem. The wrong thing to do is to argue with her about her standards – "oh you're too hard on yourself." (Unless she's fishing for compliments because her boyfriend has been hinting that she's gaining weight, in which case I'd exit the conversation if I agree with the boyfriend). The core of someone is their standards, and if you want to humiliate someone, belittle their standards.

Be Kind, Not Nice

From dictionary.com:

> "Nice" is defined as "pleasing; agreeable; delightful", while "kind" is defined as "having, showing, or proceeding from benevolence."

A nice person will lie to his barber about the shitty haircut he got from him for the sake of being agreeable. A kind person will risk the ire of his barber by being honest when asked how he likes it. The former ensures the barber will never improve. The latter makes improvement possible if the barber too is a kind, rather than nice, person. Kind people try to improve the world, while nice people want the world to approve of them.

Here's my definition of "nice people": those who are petty, innocuous, and unoriginal. Petty because they get worked up about trivialities like what someone thinks of them or the name of a restaurant (e.g. Soup NAZI Kitchen). Innocuous because they go out of their way to be inoffensive (because they seek approval, not because they're capable of entering another's spirit), which makes them a skittish bunch. Unoriginal because they follow scripts rather than read the situation.

They're the ones who ask, without sincerity, "how are you?" And get offended if the other person doesn't play along by responding honestly: "why do you ask?" or "horny, wanna fuck?" Nice people hate it when someone breaks script because they believe good manners is about following a script, little else. Breaking script exposes them for who they are: soulless frauds.

My definition of "kind": someone who risks being mean – offensive -- to make improvement possible. Steve Jobs may have been an asshole, but people worked for him because he was kind enough to push them to their limits. Same with Anna Wintour, of *Devil Meets Prada* editor of Vogue magazine fame. How about every professional coach at the highest level?

It's difficult to be kind because it involves risk. "Oh no, what if I offend that person?" "What if that person becomes angry at *me*?" I've had to train some of my customers to *return* something they don't like because it doesn't do my customer, employees, or business any good by not calling out a fuck up. Some get that but prefer to tell me than confront the employee. That helps, but it's nowhere as effective as having the customer approach the employee on the spot. People tend to forget their mistakes quickly, telling someone about their fuck up a day later isn't effective.

Kind people don't care about what others think of them. Their focus is on doing a good job and improving on that job. Nice people follow rules to avoid punishment, kind people principles to achieve results. Rules are imposed externally and must be obeyed to avoid punishment, whereas principles are internal, and inspire you to do what you think it is right or correct. That's why nice people waste time being defensive, while kind people pursue truth.

Here's an application question I ask, how would you answer it?

> *Your daughter loves gymnastics and is about to enter her first meet. She's confident about winning and even thought about the perfect place to hang her blue ribbon. While she did well, she didn't medal, and was devastated. What do you, as a parent, tell her?*

> a) Tell her you thought she was the best
> b) Tell her she has the ability and will surely win next time.
> c) Tell her she doesn't deserve to win because she didn't work hard enough.

Nice people – those with "good manners" - pick A. Liars pick B, they'll tell you that your new haircut looks good no matter what. Kind people answer C. Most applicants answer A or B, which means I wouldn't hire them to manage. A manager's job is to make people perform better rather than feel better, short-term. Let's examine the psychology behind each pick.

Answer A might involve lying, let's give respondents the benefit of the doubt and assume they're not, that they're just biased. It hints at narcissism, as her daughter's goal might not be to gain her mother's adulation, but to win first place at the competition. If that's in fact the case, then this mother cares less about what her daughter wants and more about getting her to stop feeling dejected immediately. She believes that her job as a parent is to protect her child from all emotional and physical harm. What could possibly go wrong?[22]

Those who choose answer B have no problems with lying. I suspect most of them are compulsive liars, usually to make themselves and others feel better, short-term. I ask them, "what if you're wrong and your daughter doesn't win the next time? Will she think you're a liar and never trust you again?" Those who answer B don't think about such consequences because they're impulsive, they think short-term – make daughter feel better now so I feel better now and I'm too lazy to figure out and implement a remedy for what went wrong – rather than anticipate a likely worst-case scenario: daughter loses again. Answer B also emphasizes talent over hard work, thereby relinquishing responsibility over losing. Nice people hate being responsible for failure.

Those who pick C – the kind – understand that victory is an arduous task that requires working harder and longer than the competition. Talent

---

[22] Search "Megan trailer" on YouTube to see.

isn't mentioned, winners don't leave room for lame excuses. Choice C sounds mean to nice people, but it's the only option that gives the daughter a chance to make it to the next level. She either quits or gathers herself to work harder than ever. Option C is what Michael Jordan's mother chose after he was cut, as a sophomore, from his high school varsity basketball team (nearly all pro players make varsity as freshmen).

Chapter 11
Awkward Situations

Anglo cultured folks, unless they're Rednecks, get embarrassed easily. That's why Anglo etiquette books often have a chapter on awkward situations. So we should have one too.

This chapter is different from the ones found in other etiquette books. We deal with typical situations considered elsewhere, and novel ones never discussed, as far as I know. For instance, what do you do when someone (not Black) blurts the N-word while rapping along to a song? How should you respond when someone mansplains or calls you by the wrong pronoun?

Fashion Faux Pas

Q: Someone's zipper is down. What should I do?
A: Zip it up for him without saying anything. (Less is more, show don't tell).

Q: I got a visible boner through my shorts in yoga class because of a hot chick in front of me. I was so embarrassed!
A: Fall into child's pose. If that doesn't get your pecker soft, thread the needle. That should move the blood away from your pecker. Then move your yoga mat somewhere where you can't see her and continue class.

Q: A co-worker unexpectedly got her period and her pants are bloody around the crotch. Should I say something to her?
A: Yes. If you can, offer her something like a sweater she can tie around her waist.

Q: Girlfriend asks if I like her new dress. I don't. What should I say?

72

A: Tell her she looks better naked. If that's not true, then break-up.

Everyday Weirdness

Q: I forgot someone's name. What should I do?
A: Ask the person for name. Preface it with an apology for forgetting.

Q: Someone keeps calling me by a wrong name. Should I say something about it?
A: If it bothers you, yes. Just say "My name is...".

Q: How do I remind someone they owe me money?
A: Post the reminder on their social media so his/her friends/subscribers can see it. She didn't forget, okay?

Race

Q: What do I do if a White person shows up at Halloween party in black face?
A: Ask how he/she'd feel if a Black person were to show up in white face.

Q: I have a white colleague who likes to brag to other black people about how she has a black boyfriend and is therefore one of them, even though it seems to make black people uncomfortable to hear that. Should I ask her to stop?
A: No, it's not your problem that she has jungle fever. Stay out of trouble that doesn't affect you.

Q: A White colleague brought in fried chicken and watermelon to our office potluck. What should I say to him so he never does this again?
A: Ask him how he'd like it if a Black person were to bring a kale salad.

Q: My White friends showed up at Halloween party dressed in yellowface! What should I do?

73

A: Make ching chong noises and tell them go to back to China.

Q: You catch your friend, while rapping to a song, say the word "nigger."
What do I say to him?
A: Tell him to buy nigger passes at www.niggerpasses.com. Then he can
say the n-word without remorse or fear of retribution.

Q: I'm Asian and some White person greeted me, "hey Chinaman." I'm
offended, how should I respond?
A: Call him "Hey Whiteman!" You're even now.

Relationships

Q: So my guy starts mansplaining to me yet again...
A: Cuntsplain back and you're even.

Q: My doctor keeps referring to me by my wrong pronoun, even though
I've asked him to stop doing so. What should I do, he's been my doctor
for 20 years so I don't want to find a more socially enlightened one.
A: Call him "mister" instead of "doctor."

Sex

Q: I bring back this woman for sex and she suddenly gets a bad case of
diarrhea – it won't end, she's stuck on the toilet. I don't want to fuck her
anymore but I'm still horny. What should I do?
A: Spray some potpourri in the bathroom and have her suck your dick
while she finishes pooping.

Q: He's too drunk to get it up and I'm horny.
A: Have him eat you out. Then get him drunk enough to pass out. Paint
his face with makeup, take photos, and your evening is salvaged! Posting
photos on social media is recommended.

Q: How do I, a woman, tell a guy I met online to not sit next to me in the booth on the first date after he does so? It's so creepy!
A: Tell him he'll get a better view of your tits if he sits across from you.

Q: Drunk woman asks me to kiss her but I don't want to. What should I do to not offend her?
A: Tell her you don't want to kiss her. Then get her passed out drunk so she doesn't remember what you told her. Smear her lipstick a bit and pull down her panties so she thinks she got some when she wakes up. (Does this count as lying)?

Q: Woman keeps asking me to slap her ass hard. That's fine, but after awhile, my hand hurts. How do I stop without looking like a wimp?
A: You couldn't find anything that resembles a paddle? Come on, now...fuck smart, not hard.

Chapter 12
Restaurant Etiquette

Going to a restaurant is like visiting a foreign country, each has their own rules of conduct. Every restaurant has its own ordering system, or perhaps a dress-code, or rules regarding split checks and substitutions. Don't go to McDonald's if you expect a server to take your order at your table, right? Don't go to Canlis if you want to wear sweats to dinner. If you don't like how a restaurant operates, don't go (or don't go back), just as you'd avoid certain nations as travel destinations because you don't like their laws and customs. Don't chew gum in Singapore, okay? Similarly, once you're in a restaurant, follow their rules, just as you'd expect guests to follow the rules of your home. Keep in mind that restaurants have their own reasons for operating as they do, even if you don't understand them.

Greetings

The reason why I prefer Asian restaurants is that they don't greet you, unless it's a Japanese restaurant and they don't greet you with a stupid question. They just say, "irasshai!," which means welcome. At my favorite pho spot, I walk in and someone points at a table, asks me "medium or small," and that's it. I've gone through an entire meal at my favorite dim sum place without saying a word to my server because I order off a piece of paper provided. I prefer this because there's no phoniness and wasted time, just good food and efficient service. There was an American restaurant, one of my favorites – Elemental – that had a similarly minimalistic service. They greeted you not with words, but a glass of champagne, and wouldn't respond if talked to. This pissed a lot of people off, and garnered them a devoted following.

At most restaurants in the US, you'll be greeted with "Hi, how are you today?" Don't lie because if you do, you're training your brain that lying is acceptable and normal. Often, I respond honestly with "I'm hungry." That usually elicits a smile from the host.

Ordering

- Don't hesitate to ask questions if you're not sure what you want. Most restaurants want to serve you well.

- Don't ask what's the most popular unless it's a mainstream restaurant and you have mainstream taste. You might end up with rabbit kidneys and liver salad, one of the most popular dishes at a renowned restaurant in the tourist district of Quebec City.

- Don't ask what the server's favorites are. You're you, and she's she. What you like might not be what she likes.

- Do ask the server to explain anything you're curious about and not familiar with.

- Do tell the server your preferences if you want him to pick something out for you.

Ordering at Asian Restaurants

At some (authentic) Asian restaurants, it's your job to call them over to take your order and to resolve an issue. Raise your hand so they see you and yell at them with something like "hey!" In Korean, it's "yogoyi!,' which means "over here!" Comes off rude to Anglos, not at all to Asians. The advantages of this kind of service is that your meal isn't constantly interrupted by servers asking you "if everything is ok." The French are similarly unobtrusive, they mostly stay out of your way. That's why French restaurants leave a bottle of water that you pour yourself and you have to ask them for the check. I prefer that, I find servers constantly coming over to pour water and asking if everything is ok annoying, especially when I'm in a middle of a conversation. I want my server to stay out of my space unless I call them for something.

Authentic Asian and French restaurants don't put up a muppet act, there's no pretense. Servers see their jobs as taking your order and bringing out your food, and the good ones will advise you on what to order too, if that's what you want. They're not going to ask you how your day has been, because they don't care unless maybe you're a regular and you've developed a relationship with them. You think the American server whom you've never met and who asks about your day cares? Usually not, they're just trying to be polite.

It's also acceptable for Asian and French servers to argue with you. Examples, from two of many experiences at a highly rated Chinese restaurant in Vancouver, BC, where there are so many Chinese that Chinese servers rarely adapt to Anglo manners:

> Me: this isn't chicken consommé. It's chicken broth.
> Server: (scowls at me and points at bowl of broth) this is high class food! (storms off).

> Me: I told you to not bring the desert until after the meal.
> Server: (twisted face looking at me) but you ordered it! (walks away)

The French are similar, they'll argue with you. Not like this, they'll be concerned if their consommé isn't up to par (Chinese restaurant back then would call something it's not just because it sounds fancier). But they'll treat you as your spouse treats you. Don't take it personally and give it back as you see fit – treat others as they treat you -- that's good fucking manners.

Table Manners

According to some Anglo etiquette experts, this is how you're supposed to drink soup. Summary of steps:

1. Position your body two hand widths away from the table
2. Use correct spoon, the one with the largest bowl
3. Spoon soup at and toward twelve o'clock side of bowl using the outer edge of spoon. (Am I losing you)?
4. Gently scrape off soup that's on the bottom of the spoon along the twelve o'clock edge of the bowl.
5. Bring edge of spoon that faces you to mouth without spilling or hunching over.
6. Sip soup without making noise
7. Repeat process, inserting a chopstick up the ass each time.

Don't eat with chopsticks up your ass. Instead, do what makes eating easiest, including:

- Bringing bowl to mouth
- Slurping
- Using whichever utensil you want
- Using your hands
- Licking your plate (a fine dining restaurant in Seattle, *Art of the Table*, encouraged this at their original location).

Other

Don't ask for split checks. Sort out who owes what among yourselves, every extra ticket adds 1-2 minutes of work for your server. Imagine a table of 10 asking for separate checks, how would that affect service for the entire restaurant? Don't waste other people's time over something you can easily sort out on your own.

Calling in an order at a restaurant

If it's busy at my restaurant and the first thing I hear from a calling customer who doesn't hear my greeting -- "Soup Nazi Kitchen, place you order" -- is: Hi, how are you?", I hang up on them. From 13 years of experience, I've learned that this person is going to take too much of my time so she's not worth having as a customer.

First, don't follow a script because it'll keep you from listening. This applies not only to restaurants, but to anyone you interact with. Sure, 80% of the people you interact with will follow a script that you've memorized so don't need to listen to, but remain alert for those who aren't script followers, they want efficiency because time is money. Put simply, pay attention. After all, the restaurant is paying attention to you. (If it isn't, don't go back).

Write out your order before you place it so time isn't wasted bumbling around. Don't hesitate to ask questions, restaurant don't mind you asking questions that are useful, they want to help you. They just hate it when time is wasted when they're slammed.

Don't hesitate to ask the person taking your order to repeat the order to you so you can check for accuracy. Too many restaurants take orders without knowing how to do it correctly – repeating back to customer what they hear.

Chapter 13
How to Talk to Customers

Every job involves working with customers, someone is paying you for your work. You need to know how to talk to customers if you want to achieve your goals.

Talk to customers as a courtesan would to her benefactor. Or you could talk to them as some street skank whore does to her john; or as some $300/hour escort to her client. Think about the differences between the three:

> Whore: fucks a lot of guys each day to get her drugs.

> Escort: fucks a few guys and listens to them complain about stupid shit a few times a week to pay for living expenses and a few luxuries.

> Courtesan: fucks a few guys per year she advises on marital, political and business matters.

Which of the above do you want to be? You want your customers to be benefactors, clients, or johns? You want to live in a world where there's a good chance someone's going to knock your rotting teeth out or where you don't have to worry about being murdered on the job? Do you want to live a life where your opinion matters? So you better start practicing now because the courtesans have been working on their game ever since they could talk and walk.

What's the only difference between a street whore and an escort? The former has a drug habit for way too long. What's the difference between an escort and a courtesan? The former is a narcissist. Notice I haven't mentioned anything about looks because as long as the body's bangin', that's mostly irrelevant.

Know Your Customer

What do most people like to talk about the most? Pick:

a) Ideas
b) Other people
c) Themselves

Correct answer is C. Narcissism is our Original Sin and your job is to figure out how to curb your own narcissistic urges so you can turn the customer into your benefactor (what most want to be) instead of a john (what most are). Put simply, your job is to seduce those we want as customers and to repel the shitheads.

Pick:

a) Treat others as you want to be treated
b) Treat others as they treat you
c) Treat others as they want to be treated

Those who pick A are intolerant narcissists because they project their wants and needs onto other people, they don't realize that other people have different preferences and perspectives from their own. Those who pick A can only have friends who are copies of themselves because any deviance from their narrow worldview offends their sense of self and righteousness. Repel these people, they're dangerous. They color themselves with righteous sounding identities such as "social justice warrior" and "human rights activist" to hide the fact that they're totalitarians and liars.

If you picked B, then you've picked up on psychological mirroring, which is how you achieve "greater connection and understanding with the individual who is being mirrored."[23] Mirroring requires empathy, which is not the same as sympathy (i.e. narcissists acting nice), and empathy involves seeing something from different perspectives. Those who pick B are also good at protecting themselves from being used because they give off vibe that they will retaliate in kind to protect themselves.

---

[23] https://en.wikipedia.org/wiki/Mirroring

Those who pick C are capable of empathy, but incapable of protecting themselves.

How to Talk to Customers, Anyone Really

Now that you know who the shitheads are — at my place, they often refuse to follow Ordering Guidelines because they wrongly assume employees are as incompetent as they are (narcissistic projection) — you can focus on providing the best service possible to your customers without violating your integrity. All prostitutes have boundaries.

Never Say "No" to Customers

"No" creates a communication barrier. Always maintain a we-can-do-it-all atmosphere. Figure out a way to provide what the customer wants (without violating your integrity).

Like restauranteur Cameron Mitchell's "The Answer is Yes. What's the Question" policy. His milkshake story:

> Mitchell was celebrating his son's birthday at a restaurant. His son wants a chocolate milkshake, so they ask the server for one. Server tells them that they don't *offer* milkshakes.
>
> Mitchell asks, "Do you have milk? Do you have chocolate ice cream? Do you have a blender? Well, you can make a chocolate milkshake." The server asks the manager, but the answer is the same: no milkshake because it's not on the menu.

The answer was "no" because the server and manager were obedient, not responsible. They followed rules because they were afraid to make and to take responsibility for their mistakes. As long as they follow the rules, they can blame someone else if the customer doesn't have a good experience.

Ultimately, executive management is to blame for Mitchell's bad experience. They're the ones who set company guidelines and policies and oversee training of floor staff. Their leadership failed to give employees the confidence to be responsible and make thoughtful decisions.

In any case, someone told Mitchell that the exact same thing had happened to him—at one of Mitchell's own restaurants. That infuriated Mitchell. He has since made sure that every new employee hears the "Milkshake Story" first day of training. "We want our people to have the attitude, 'The answer is yes. What's the question?'" he says. This simple philosophy is one of the reasons Mitchell's restaurants take regular customers and turn them into raving fans.

Those with good fucking manners don't say "no." "No" makes people shut down, it creates unnecessary communication barriers, and it prevents you from figuring out a way to get shit done despite obstacles. Examples:

> New Customer: Do you have strawberries?
> Obedient Employee: No, we don't.
> New Customer: Oh, ok. Do you have blueberries?
> Obedient Employee: Nope.
> New Customer: Ok. I'll stop by some other time.

Versus someone who has good fucking manners.

> New Customer: Do you have strawberries?
> Responsible Employee: We're seasonal so we'll have them soon. Are you looking for something fruity?
> New Customer: Mmmm, yeah.
> Responsible Employee: Do you like mangoes because they smell and look great today?
> New Customer: Yeah, I like mangoes.
> Responsible Employee: How about the Tropical Bugs bunny. It has mangoes, pineapple, banana and a bit of carrot juice, which brings out the mango and pineapple flavors.
> New Customer: Okay, I'll take that.
> Responsible Employee: How is it?
> New Customer: So good. Thank you!

Those with good fucking manners have a high ask-to-talk ratio. Asking questions invites customer to talk, to work with you to come up with a solution. Another example:

> Customer: Do you sell milkshakes?
> Good manners: No, sorry.
> Customer: Oh, ok.

versus good fucking manners:

> Customer: Do you sell milkshakes?
> Responsible: We have something better and tastes just like it. Would you like to try it?
> Customer: What's it called? What's in it?
> Responsible: It's an avocado milkshake. It has avocado, peanut butter, some kale, and your choice of fruit — I recommend apple — and whey protein. It tastes just like a milkshake but it's so much healthier, guaranteed.
> Customer: Hmmm, ok. I'll try it.
> Responsible: Great...here you go.
> Customer: Omigosh, it really is like a milkshake! Thank you so much!!!

Those with good fucking manners understand that their customer isn't ordering a milkshake, he's asking for a feeling. He wants something — taste, texture, maybe color — that will remind him of happy times, perhaps memorable childhood events. The milkshake is irrelevant. Those with good fucking manners will be able to re-create the milkshake, give the customer the feeling he wants.

Ask Questions

Two to three is best, anymore and some get annoyed. When you ask someone a question about themselves, you make that person feel less lonely. Most people are lonely because most people prefer to talk about themselves than ask questions, which means few are listening. (Hermits, ironically, are the least lonely because they haven't lost the ability — a rich inner world — to keep themselves company). A customer you make feel less lonely becomes your benefactor. It's not hard to pull off. Here's an example of an uncivilized conversation:

> You: Whom did you vote for?
> Customer: Trump
> You: You're an ignorant racist!
> Customer: Hey fuck you.

Never rush to judgment and conclusion, you'll never learn and grow if you do that. Here's how to have the same conversation the civilized way

> You: Whom did you vote for?
> Customer: Trump
> You: Why did you vote for him?
> Customer: I like that he wants to get the US out of foreign engagements we have no business being in and I like that he promises to protect US steel industry because that's a matter of national security. We need to have a robust steel industry in cas we go to war...
> You: Interesting, I never thought of it that way, thanks for the insight. Do you think Trump is a racist?
> Customer: Not any more than any of the other candidates. He' just more uncensored and I care more about results than insults.

Always ask at least two follow up questions. (Again, too many and you' annoy some people so watch for that). The more questions you ask, the closer you'll get to the truth. Another uncouth conversation:

> You: How are you?
> Customer: I'm fine. How are you?
> You: Omigod, my math professor is such a stupid jerk off. Can you believe he doesn't give partial credit? Who does that? I mean, I'm really good at Math, I got straight As in it in high school and now I have a C. How is that possible? Don't you think there's something wrong with him?

That's how skanks talk — mostly about themselves and their own stupid problems. Few people care about your problems. Many will pretend to care. An escort, for instance, talks to show solidarity with and sympathy for her customer. Example:

> Customer: my son is having a lot of problems at school.
> You: I'm sorry. Boys are really tough to deal with at that age. He'll grow out of it, I'm sure.

A courtesan, on the other hand, talks to solve other people's problems. That's why she probes and suggests solutions. Example:

> Customer: my son is having a lot of problems at school.
> You: What sort of problems?
> Customer: drugs, not doing his schoolwork. He's close to flunking out.
> You: Why is he doing those things?
> Customer: Not sure. He could be bored, he doesn't learn the way they want him to learn.
> You: Would you consider a boarding school that's better suited for his learning style?
> Customer: Maybe. Tell me more...

This conversation gives customer an opportunity to get beyond ranting, to think about solutions to his problem. The courtesan's value is in her usefulness, not her sex.

Avoid Banalities and Cliches

Make yourself stand out. If everyone else is asking: "Hi, how are you?" then find another question to ask. "Where are you going?," for instance. Example:

> You: Where are you going after this?
> Customer: Checking out a wedding venue.
> You: You getting married?
> Customer: Yes!
> You: Do you have a caterer?
> Customer: No, why do you ask?
> You: We've catered weddings. Can we put a bid in?
> Customer: Absolutely!

Asking people *what* they're doing will generate more business and social opportunities. Another example:

> You: What do you do for work?
> Customer: I'm a structural engineer.
> You: Hey, I'm majoring in Physics to become a structural engineer. Do you have internships?
> Customer: We do. Have a resume ready by Friday and I'll stop in to look at it.
> You: Awesome, will do. Thanks!

See why some people have all the luck? These people live a different routine from those who have no luck or bad luck. You're responsible for your own karma.

Don't Lie to the Customer

There are few instances where lying is justified. We're not going to get into those because most people in America are compulsive liars. It's a polite nation and that's not good.

Anyway, learn to say: "I don't know."

That's what intelligent people say when they don't know something because they're aware of and comfortable with their ignorance. Don't make random guesses, life isn't a multiple-choice exam and it makes you look stupid. It's ok to guess if you let the customer know that you're making an educated guess.

Never Say What You Don't Mean

Even when a customer says hi to you with an insincere and trite greeting — "How are you?" when they mean to say "hi" — don't just play along to be polite — "I'm fine, thank you. How are you?" — if that's not how you feel. Compulsive lying begins with seemingly benign little lies. Batshit crazy also begins with thinking that everything needs to be a-ok all the time and with suppressing your emotions. Engaging in scripted politeness will also train you to not listen when people talk. Don't let these savages destroy your life. Alternative responses to the insincere version of "How are you?":

- "Dunno, haven't thought about it."
- "Why do you ask?"
- Ignore the question.

Or answer honestly. It could be "I'm fine." Could also be:

- "I'm angry. I want to beat the shit out of someone."
- "I'm really confused because my boyfriend told me something last night that came out of nowhere yada yada yada...."

Don't let customers violate your integrity. Don't lie about stupid shit because if you do, you'll soon start lying about all sorts of shit out of habit and that'll get you in a lot of trouble.

Be Precise and Say Less

The more you say, the less people will understand and trust you. Say only what needs to be said. Say what you have to say in as few words as possible to minimize misunderstanding and sounding like a rambling idiot. Example of customer service at Alive Juice Bar:

> Customer: What do you do with the juice fiber?
> Bad Answer: Well, we generally just throw out most of it. Some of it though we'll use to make the raw carrot cake desert. We'll also use it in the avocado salad.
> Good Answer: (pointing to fridge) Carrot cake and avocado salads.

The good answer will result in more customers exploring other products. Bad answer will confuse most customers. Keep it simple. Less is more, less is best.

Control Customer Perception and Expectations

Customer perception and expectations are as important as the products themselves. It's similar to psychological framing, my definition:

89

The framing effect is an example of cognitive bias, in which people react to a particular choice in different ways depending on how it is presented...

Much of customer perceptions and expectations are framed by the décor (how you dress, where you live, what car you drive), prices (how much you charge for your services), and online marketing (e.g. Yelp reviews, Facebook updates). People are more impressed with a puny guy dressed like a dork who kicks big boy ass than Hulk Hogan doing the same. People expect to pay high prices when they enter a fancy looking restaurant.

You also frame by how you describe your products. Never use superlatives — "tastes incredible," for instance — to describe products, and that includes yourself (you are one). Taste is subjective so that's for the customer to decide. Just describe the flavor and texture profile of a product. Reference familiar flavors and textures. Example:

> Bad: "The Supermodel tastes great and will make you look like a Supermodel, guaranteed!"
> Good: It's a protein shake that's a salad and it tastes like green tea ice cream.

"Green tea ice cream" instead of "tastes great," so the customer can decide if they like the flavor profile. If you insist that your product tastes great and the customer doesn't agree, then the customer will either not trust you or label you a liar. So don't oversell your products, your customers will be disappointed more often when you do. Play the slow game instead. Be modest, never boastful. The sales will come as long as you keep improving your products because people are more impressed with improvements than the actual product. It's heartening to watch people and businesses grow.

Be Dignified

If a customer treats you poorly, it's your fault not the customer's. Only undignified people blame others when treated poorly. The dignified blame themselves and take steps to ensure it never happens again.

Avoid the temptation to play victim, it'll dis-empower you and turn you into an ill-mannered and disrespected dipshit who blames other people for your problems. When someone treats you poorly, it's because you act as if you deserve to be treated as such. It could be because you're an arrogant asshole making unreasonable requests to make yourself look and feel better. Or because you act like a doormat. In any case, be noble, that's how those with good fucking manners act. From one of my application questions, pick:

> Someone mugs you. Whose fault is it that you were mugged?
> a) Mugger's fault
> b) Your fault
> c) Society's fault

Leftist lemmings pick C. Kookie conservatives pick A. Noble people pick B. The moment you think like a victim is the moment you lose control of your destiny and become a victim. The predators can smell a prey who deserves to be eaten.

Be Commanding

If you can tell that a customer doesn't like something, *command* them to return it and fix it to their liking. Don't ask them if they want you to fix it because they would've asked you to do so already had they good fucking manners. Those with good manners prefer to lie: "no, it's fine" when it's not because they think it's rude to say otherwise. So you have to *command* them to do what's best for them. Say "bring it here, I'll fix it." And resist the urge to call that person a "passive-aggressive fucktard" as you fix the problem.

Chapter 14
Bad Manners

American obsession with the politeness of their greetings and requests comes at the expense of calling out or noticing truly appalling behavior. It's as if every "please" and "thank you" muttered absolves one of egregious sins committed with casual frequency. Here are some example of bad manners that are rarely mentioned.

Gotcha questions

Also known as loaded questions. A loaded question is a rhetorical device in that it that doesn't actually seek answers. Instead, it expresses the questioner's own opinions, assumptions, prejudices, or even lies in the hope that such elements will be taken for granted. For example:

- "Why do you think it's acceptable to waste so much money on frivolous things?"

This question assumes that the person being asked wastes money on frivolous things and that there's an objective standard of what is and isn' frivolous. It also implies that spending money on enjoyable or non-essential items is unacceptable or wrong. By asking the question in this way, the person asking the question tries to put the other person on the defensive by assuming something negative about them. A more neutral way to phrase the question:

- "Why did you buy that?"

This question shows that the questioner has an open mind – she recognizes that what may be frivolous to her may not be to another. Some people think that pedicures are frivolous. Others see it as a way to prevent athlete's foot and to improve blood circulation, it's a health matter similar to visiting the dentist for a cleaning. In any case, this question invites the responder to explain his perspective without being defensive. And it's not that those with good fucking manners don't judge, they do but they either suspend judgment until they've asked a few questions, or they keep their judgement to themselves.

Here's another example:

- "How can you be so evil and stupid to support such a despicable policy?"

This question is loaded because it implies that this "policy" is in fact despicable and attacks the character of anyone who supports it. It tries to put the responder on the defensive because defensive behavior isn't attractive. This type of loaded question is often used in political discourse to attack opponents or to push a specific agenda. (Which is why those with good fucking manners tend to be either apolitical or quietly so).

Those with good fucking manners would instead ask:

- "Why do you support this policy?"

There's no judgment of character, but there's a sense of wonder in this question. Again, there's nothing wrong with judging people and if after hearing the supporting arguments you conclude that the arguments are dumb, don't hesitate to call the answerer a dumbfuck. Those with good fucking manners exercise patience, but not necessarily restraint.

Here's one that teenagers say to each other:

- "You bought that to look cool, eh?"

It's a passive aggressive way to express contempt, that this person isn't cool and therefore has to try to be so.

How to Respond to Loaded Questions

Resist the urge to beat the shit out of the person who asks you a loaded question, not because it's immoral and bad manners to do so – it's not -- but because it's illegal and may land you in jail. (Though it's been said that a few years in jail can be good for personal growth). At any rate, here are some additional tips on how to reply to a loaded question:

1. Don't be defensive. Often, the first urge is to be defensive. "But I don't spend money on frivolous things!" one is tempted to say. Defensiveness smacks of insecurity and guilt. Say instead and perhaps: "What sort of frivolous things do I buy?" By responding to the questions with such a question, you show that you...

2. Acknowledge the questioner's perspective, always, even if you disagree with it. First, people love to be acknowledged, you'll take the edge off the conversation when you do this. Second, you might learn something about yourself by doing so, other people notice things about you that you don't. Finally, you shift the burden of proof off yourself and onto the questioner.

3. Ask questions that make the questioner consider his prejudices and assumptions. "Why do you think my weekly pedicures are frivolous?"

4. Ask about the questioner's motivation is for asking the question. No, not "why the fuck do you care?", that's defensive and combative. And don't identify the question as loaded, just say "why do you ask?" At this point, they're forced to hide their primary intention – to humiliate you – and babble on about how they have your best interest in mind. Thank them for caring so much.

5. Acknowledge that the questioner is right if she is, it's thanking them for giving you valuable insight about yourself. "You're right, I should spend less on Funko toys." Resist the urge to follow that up with dismissal: "but whatever, I still like shopping at Funko." That's something you can say to someone who is merely curious about your habits, not to someone who wants to humiliate and dominate you.

6. Don't mention to the questioner that she's wrong if she is. She already knows she's wrong, don't waste time by rubbing it in.

7. Don't try to change people's minds. Don't get into arguments, they're a waste of time. State your case and if the questioner disagrees, shut up.

The above can be practiced in private. Most people have heard such loaded questions, you can replay them and act out how you'd like it to go. Think of it as theater practice.

Other Gotcha Questions

Asking a question and then answering them yourself in the form of another question, as if seeking to confirm your own conclusions.

> "So why did you go to Thailand? It's because you wanted to pick up cheap whores, right?"

These types of questions aren't always malicious. Someone asked me:

> "How did you get sick? It must be because you were really stressed, right?" (in a caring tone)

That's just how some people talk, they talk to themselves when they're talking to others. Resist the urge to say "no" when they're wrong. Just answer the first question and ignore the second.

Asking a question not out of curiosity but as a way to talk about oneself without coming off as self-centered. For instance:

> "Are you going on vacation this summer?"
> "Yes."
> "Oh my god, I am too! I'm going to Hawaii, and then Thailand..."

If the question is sincere, there'd be a follow up question: "Where are you going?" The questioner isn't interested in the person, she only wants to talk about herself without appearing self-centered.

If your urge to exclaim something about yourself is overwhelming, just say what you have to say. "I'm going to Harvard!" "I got a promotion!" "I'm getting married!" It's okay to talk about yourself without prompt, just don't do it all the time – limit it to major life events -- and never do a bait and switch. A bait in switch is like offering a dog a treat and then eating it yourself. It's a form of...

Conversational Narcissism

> "Check out my new dress!"
> "That's nice. I bought one too, here are some pictures of it from Friday night, how do you think I look in it?"

Conversational narcissism is a term used to describe a communication style in which one person dominates a conversation, focusing almost exclusively on themselves and their own experiences, without showing much interest or curiosity about the other person's thoughts, feelings, or experiences.

Conversational narcissists tend to steer conversations back to themselves, interrupt others, and talk over them. They may also use tactics such as one-upping, where they try to outdo the other person's experiences with their own, or hijacking the conversation to make it about themselves. Conversational narcissism can be frustrating for the other person and can make them feel unheard or unimportant. It can also lead to a lack of genuine connection and mutual understanding in the conversation.[24]

There was a couple who once opened a restaurant that quickly failed. They approached me and my then partner at a party, a few months after we'd opened our first restaurant. The conversation started with them trying to show empathy by talking about themselves.

> "Life was so difficult after we opened Qube, I know exactly how you're feeling and what you're going through. We were running around and working all the time, it was so stressful and frustrating..."

We listened. Then one of them tried to be helpful.

> "You know, you can pay money to get your bad reviews removed." (their restaurant had received many epic bad reviews)
> "But we haven't had any bad reviews yet."
> "Oh?" [blank look]

This is how a lot of "empaths" talk and think: they assume that your troubles are just like theirs. And that you feel just as they would if they were in your situation. That's why they don't bother to ask good questions.

---

[24] Entire paragraph generated by ChatGPT, 3/9/23. Keywords: "What is conversational narcissism?"

Beware of anyone -- especially self-described empaths -- who says: "I kno
exactly how you feel." That's usually the prelude to a rambling story
about how they were "once there" too.

Common acts of conversational narcissism, summarized.

1. Interrupting the other person: For example, if the other person i
    telling a story or sharing an experience, the conversational
    narcissist might interrupt them to start talking about their own
    similar experience without allowing the other person to finish
    their story.
2. One-upping: If the other person shares an experience, the
    conversational narcissist may try to top it by sharing a similar
    experience of their own, or exaggerating the details to make thei
    experience seem more impressive or interesting.
3. Hijacking the conversation: The conversational narcissist may
    change the topic of the conversation to something that they wai
    to talk about, even if it's not related to what the other person wa
    saying.
4. Bragging: The conversational narcissist may constantly talk abo
    their own accomplishments, achievements, or possessions,
    without showing much interest in the other person's life.

Overall, conversational narcissism is characterized by a lack of genuine
interest or empathy for the other person, and a strong focus on oneself.

Defensiveness

Defensive behavior refers to actions or attitudes that people adopt in
order to protect themselves from perceived threats or criticism. Here are
some examples of defensive behavior, also known as making excuses:

1. Denial: Refusing to acknowledge or accept responsibility for a mistake or a problem.
2. Blaming: Shifting responsibility for a problem or mistake onto someone else.
3. Rationalization: Justifying one's actions or decisions with seemingly plausible reasons, even if they are not entirely true.
4. Avoidance: Refusing to engage in a situation or conversation that might lead to discomfort or criticism.
5. Projection: Attributing one's own negative qualities or feelings to someone else.
6. Deflecting: Changing the subject or redirecting attention away from oneself when faced with criticism or uncomfortable questions.
7. Counter-attacking: Responding to criticism or perceived threats with aggression or hostility.
8. Minimization: Downplaying the significance of a problem or mistake, or trivializing the concerns of others.
9. Withdrawal: Shutting down emotionally or physically, and disengaging from a situation or relationship.
10. Passive aggression: Indirectly expressing anger or frustration through subtle acts of resistance or sabotage.

Defensive behaviors are unattractive for several reasons:

1. It makes communication difficult: When someone is being defensive, it can be hard to have an open and honest conversation because the defensive person may be more focused on protecting themselves than on listening and understanding.
2. It's a sign of lack of confidence: When someone is defensive, it can come across as though they are not confident in themselves or their abilities. This can be unattractive because confidence is often seen as an attractive trait.

3. It's frustrating for others: Dealing with someone who is being defensive can be frustrating, especially if the other person is trying to have a productive conversation or work together to solve a problem.

4. It creates tension and conflict: Defensive behavior can escalate a situation and create unnecessary tension and conflict, which is generally not an attractive or desirable outcome.

5. It prevents growth and progress: When someone is defensive, they may be resistant to feedback or suggestions for improvement, which can prevent them from growing and developing in their personal or professional life. This can be unattractive because it suggests that the defensive person is not open to change or improvement.

I see parents drill their kids to say "please" and "thank you" and to keep their elbows off tables but rarely do I see them flinch when their kid acts defensively, saying stupid shit like "oh, this is the first time I've made that mistake" or "relax, no harm, no foul." In fact, it has become fashionable to make excuses not only for their kids, but for everyone, especially the "marginalized," because they perversely think that it's good manners to do so. "Oh, it must be stress." "It's because of institutional racism." "Patriarchy," "heteronormativity," "I didn't grow up with money," and so forth. It's like feeding a kid candy bars for dinner and then praising them for finishing all of it. Each excuse is a candy bar, it makes you feel good short-term, sick long-term. Get making excuses out of your life to achieve your goals and to maintain robust mental health.

Stating the Obvious

What's the point? It usually comes off as condescending and rarely accomplishes anything. A few examples:

- Telling a homeless person to get a job. Would you hire this person?
- Telling an obese person to lose weight. Doctors do this all the time and it's needlessly condescending. There's no point to it because the fat person, deep down, already knows that. Better to state how the patient's obesity affects their health and leave it at that.
- Telling someone who is crying to stop crying. Crying is usually a fundamental emotional expression, it's not like the fake smiles I want to smack off people's faces. Not saying crying is always attractive, some people cry over stupid shit. But what's the point of telling someone how they should express what they're feeling? Is it healthy to repress an honest emotion?
- Saying "I told you so." You did. Do you want a candy bar for being correct?

Random Everyday Bad Manners

The ones that either happen too frequently or never get called out as bad manners.

- Taking up two parking spots, and this includes street parking.
- Hanging out at gas pump to message someone after you've filled up while there's a line of cars waiting behind you.
- Standing around blocking a path.
- Not having check-in card (e.g. for the gym, Costco) out at the right time, making people behind wait longer than necessary.
- Blocking the path on escalators. It's left-hand walking, right-hand standing.
- Not pulling ahead to let cars behind pass when turning left or right at intersection.
- Expressing an opinion on something one hasn't read/watched.

- Talking about writing a memoir despite being younger than 50 without notable accomplishments.
- Not showing up on time. I disagree that this is a matter of fashion in some cultures. I've found those who live in "fashionably late" cultures are also generally unreliable and self-absorbed. When enough people are this way, it becomes normalized as a natural and normal part of the culture. Fuck that, natural and normal or not, it's bad culture and those who play along are shitheads. Unless they're the next Bill Gates, which usually isn't the case, they're just wasting time because they can.

Virtue Signaling

It's moral grandstanding. It's the same as bragging, it's an ego boost. It's obnoxious, I want to bitch slap every virtue signaler.

I saw this posted by someone on Facebook:

- Whoever doesn't believe in HUMAN RIGHTS can UNFRIEND me now!

Lots of people approved – perhaps another example of virtue signaling? -- of this self-aggrandizing and ignorant message. Ignorant because while the idea of human rights sounds high-minded and moral, it's ultimately a Gotcha political concept. Meaning, its purpose isn't to make the world a better place, it's to spread nasty rumors about those you don't like so you have an excuse to bully and bomb them while making yourself look righteous while doing it. Listening to Westerners talk about human rights is like watching the movie *Mean Girls,* the preening and hypocrisy are breathtaking.

Fishing for Compliments

It's similar to virtue signaling, they're both roundabout ways of praising oneself. Fishing for compliments is more manipulative and tiresome because it involves baiting another person for it to work. It's another tactic used by narcissists to get a dose of admiration while trying to come off as humble and self-effacing. Example:

Person A: "I don't know if I look good in this outfit. What do you think?"
Person B: "I think you look great! That color really suits you."
Person A: "Oh, really? I wasn't sure. I feel like I look kind of frumpy today."
Person B: "No way! You always look amazing."

It's off-putting and a waste of time. But the pro-affirmation crowd encourage it even though it involves lying, manipulation, and insincerity. Does Person A ever sincerely want Person B's honest opinion or only her compliments? If Person A is lying just to fish for a compliment, can she ever be trusted? Will she make up flattering stories about herself? Is it possible to have healthy relationships where this kind of behavior is deemed good manners?

Gratuitous Compliments

"Since when did grandmothers look like college students?" writes Miss Nice on grandma's Facebook feed after she posts a picture of herself with her latest grandchild. Does this really make grandma feel better, does it help her age gracefully? Or will this remind her of wasted opportunities of her youth? Perhaps she'll reminisce about her youth instead of working to improve her present? People die not just because of age, but because they yearn for the past instead of work for the future. The best option is to not say anything because there are unintended consequences to everything you say and do. That's why less is best.

Who else gives gratuitous compliments? Unctuous salespeople and sleazy guys trying to pick up bimbos. Be on alert when you hear flattery, it means there's trouble if you let it affect your decision making. Nice people sell using flattery, while kind people sell by solving people's problems. Stay focused on winning, not on your ego. Those with good fucking manners never give or hear gratuitous compliments.

Part IV
The Purpose of Good Fucking Manners

Do not accept the roles that society foists on you. Re-create yourself by forging a new identity, one that commands attention and never bores the audience. Be the master of your own image rather than letting others define if for you. Incorporate dramatic devices into your public gestures and actions – your power will be enhanced and your character will seem larger than life.

—— **Robert Greene,** *The 48 Laws of Power*

Chapter 15
Chinese People Don't Say "Thank you"

They do, but not often, and never between close friends and relatives. Such formalities are seen as creating distance among close relations.

Chinese society is Confucian and the family, not the individual, is the basic unit in such societies. "Thank you" implies an exchange between two individuals. Chinese families don't consist of individuals in the Western sense, so it's seen as ridiculous for a daughter to thank her father for doing something he's supposed to do (duty). And saying "thank you" to a family member is like saying it to yourself – there aren't personal boundaries between family members, everything belongs to everyone, there's no "mine" and "yours." A mother doesn't see her kids as individuals separate from her, she sees them as extensions of herself. The Chinese family would break down if the mother thanked her son for doing the dishes because it implies that he's a separate entity from the family who has a choice in the matter. Honor and duty, not respect for individual liberty, is the glue that binds Chinese families together. It's like being in the military, it's not for everyone.

Outside of the family, saying "thank you" is still problematic. In Confucian societies, gratitude highlights the unequal status between the giver and recipient. Pong the peasant can thank Gong the governor for not burning down his village in exchange for deference, but is it necessary to thank your server for bringing your dim sum? The server, after all, is doing her job (duty) and why would a customer to defer to her when the exchange is transactional, food for money? If anyone should say "thank you," it'd be the server because the customer doesn't have to eat at her restaurant. For a customer to thank the server would undermine the importance of social hierarchy and the idea that individuals have roles and responsibilities based on their position in society. It'd disrupt social harmony.

And finally, "thank you" implies "I owe you" and that the person receiving the thanks has done something exceptional or gone out of their way to help, which can create a sense of indebtedness or obligation that neither party is comfortable with. If they are, then "thank you" is said and the debt is expected to be repaid.

This approach to manners isn't unique to China or Confucian societies, something similar goes on in India, where Hindi culture is similarly family-centered and collectivistic.

> *In India, people—especially when they are your elders, relatives, or close friends—tend to feel that by thanking them, you're violating your intimacy with them and creating formality and distance that shouldn't exist. They may think that you're closing off the possibility of relying on each other in the future.*[25]

The point of this chapter isn't to extol the virtues of Chinese society and to shit on American etiquette. It's to point out that while etiquette exists in all societies – and for different reasons -- manners aren't universal. A "thank you" in America might mean something different in another society. Never assume the naturalness and universality of your manners, not everyone wants to play along. That's good fucking manners, especially when you travel abroad.

Americans should express gratitude – say "thank you" -- more often than the Chinese because it makes sense to do so in a society that's focused on individual liberty instead of roles and responsibilities, and that's cool, I don't want to upend the basis of American life. But Americans tend to be linguistically careless. Like the woman who says "literally" every other sentence for emphasis rather than meaning. Similarly, those with "good

---

[25] https://www.theatlantic.com/international/archive/2015/06/thank-you-culture-india-america/395069/

manners" will say "thank you" like a parrot with Tourette's syndrome. Makes me wonder if they're hiding something vile about themselves. Or are they being sarcastic, like the police officer saying "thank you" after handing someone a ticket? Are they trying to prove that they're well-mannered through words instead of action? If any of those are the case, cut down on bizarre verbal tics and be more judicious and appropriate in your choice of words if you want to have good fucking manners. Less is more and less is the best.

> *After moving to America, it took me several years to say thanks to people without actually meaning it. Putting "thank you" on the tip of my tongue, ready to escape at a moment's notice, rather than extracting it from the depths of my heart, was one of the hardest language lessons I had to learn in the United States.*[26]

Those with good manners say "thank you" out of habit and because they were taught to do so. Those with good fucking manners say it because they mean it.

---

[26] *Ibid.*

Chapter 16
Devil in the Kitchen

Chapter One. Marco Pierre White, when his maître d' fucks up a cheese plate:

> *I picked up the first cheese. "Not right!" With all my might I threw it against the wall. It stuck to the tiles. I picked up the second cheese "Not right! I chucked it at the wall. Then I hurled the remaining cheese, one after another, at that wall.*
>
> *Nicolas and a couple of cooks raced over to the wall, ready to pry off the cheese and clear up the smelly mess. I shouted, "Leave them there. Leave them there. Leave them fucking there all night. No one is allowed to touch them." The cheese had to stay on that wall all night so that whenever Nicolas came into the kitchen, he would see them glued to the white tiles and would never, ever make the mistake again.*

What makes a great cook, who becomes a great chef? What drives someone to work 17-hour days, six days a week? Marco Pierre White's memoir, *Devil in the Kitchen: Sex, Pain, and Madness* answers these questions. Read it if you want to be a better cook. Read it if you want a career in the restaurant industry. Read it if you're stupid enough to consider quitting your well-paying job to pursue your dream of owning a restaurant. Read it if you want to enter the mind of the Devil. Read it if you want to be the Devil.

White is considered the first post-modern rock star chef, and the youngest ever, at age 33, to win three Micheline stars. He's Big Daddy O, a big fucking deal. We owe him (and Japanese food shows) the Food Network (otherwise we'd be stuck with Julia Child version 4.0 and Giada's tits). He trained some of the guys we watch on TV: Gordon Ramsay (White claims to be the only person to break him); Mario Batali (quit after White threw hot risotto at him); Curtis Stone; Heston Blumenthal, the list goes on. Lots of Micheline stars. So how did he do it? His words:

You have to deliver the message that they must never take a shortcut. You can't just say, "Come on, boys, let's try to get it right." That just won't work. If you are not extreme, then peopl will take shortcuts because they don't fear you. And to achieve and retain the very highest standards, day after day, meal after meal, in an environment as difficult and fast as a restaurant kitchen, is extreme, well, in the extreme.

Put simply: fear, respect, love. In that order.

Fear

White is a master at instilling fear because he's able to enter people's spiri He has extraordinary observation skills. White biographer Bill Buford notes that though White dropped out of school at 16 — he was labeled a dumbass because of his dyslexia — and has always had difficulty reading, he found that White comprehends everything that's read to him: "genius level comprehension ability." What separates White from the mediocre is that he pays attention and does so for long stretches. White is thus able t learn faster and to get to know people more deeply. He's able to enter another's spirit, understand what another perceives.

Here's a rough Buford example of how White enters the spirit of an employee. White will ask him about his family, past, hopes, aspirations. From that he figures out his fears. Here's how it goes down when this employee makes excuses or complains (some artistic license):

> *White: I knew you're going to be just like your father, you fucking cunt. You're going to beat your wife just as your father beat your mother. You're going to beat your children just as he beat you. You're going to be another drunk, useless, cunt. Stan in that corner.*

But psychological terror and humiliation (he really did make employees stand in the corner, even ran out of corners once) wasn't enough. He used the threat of physical punishment to cement their fear. He turned off the AC when employees complained about the heat. He cut up the shirt and pants of an employee who complained about the heat. He threw all sorts of stuff at people, including hot risotto at Mario Batali.

Most didn't last a week in White's kitchen. But enough stayed and some of them, like Gordon Ramsay, became great chefs.

Respect

White earned respect of employees, customers, and reviewers because he didn't let any of them fuck with him. Employees respected him because he was quick to eject pain in the ass customers. Customers respected him because his employees had his back, always ready to brawl. Reviewers respected him because he didn't give a shit what they thought — returned all his Micheline stars and told them to fuck off. He stuck to his convictions and learned to not let employees, customers, and reviewers run his business. He believed in himself. He stood for something.

Love

"Those bastards can come any day and take it all away." White doesn't count on anyone to love him and resists the urge to mistake adulation for love. That's why he never lets his guard down and is always trying to improve. White also understands love as an act, not as a feeling and that loving someone is a more powerful motivator than the desire to be loved. "Every man should build a monument to his mother" (his mum died when he was 6). For White, words of love are meaningless. There must be proof, and the proof is in the monument.

While *Devil in the Kitchen* is primarily a story about how White reached the pinnacle of his profession, throughout there are snippets of advice for amateur cooks. Not recipes, he's primarily interested in teaching the proper mindset and methods.

> *Cook's brain. It's that ability to visualize the food on the plate, as a picture in the mind, and then work backwards. There's no reason why domestic cooks can't do the same thing. Cooking is easy: you've just got to think about what you are doing and why you are doing it.*

Apply the cook's brain and visualize that fried egg on the plate. Do you want it to be burned around the edges? Do you want to see craters on the egg white? Should the yolk look as if you'd need a hammer to break into it? The answer to all these questions should be no. Yet the majority of people still crack an egg and drop it into searingly hot oil and continue to cook it on high heat. You need to insert earplugs to reduce the horrific volume of the sizzle. And the result, once served up in a pool of oil, is an inedible destruction of that greatest ingredient — the egg. Maybe that's how you like it, in which case carry on serving your disgusting food.

This is how one of the greatest chefs talks to people, including his customers. This is the kind of advice that amateur and professional cooks need to improve results. For White, cooking isn't about following recipes. Cooking is reverse engineering whatever it is one wants. It's about entering another person's spirit — understanding how someone experiences what you make for them. It's about serving and pleasing other people, never the affirmation of one's ego.

Chapter 17
How Steve Jobs Made Your iPhone

Excerpts from Walter Isaacson's biography of Steve Jobs (2011).

A Different Kind of FDA

Walter Isaacson describes how Jobs handled himself when a partner wasn't performing adequately:

> VLSI Technology, a chip company, was having trouble delivering enough chips on time. Jobs stormed into a meeting and started shouting that they were "fucking dickless assholes." The company ended up getting the chips to Apple on time, and its executives made jackets that boasted on the back, "Team FDA."

"You guys don't know what you're doing!"

> When Apple was about to reveal the "Bondi Blue" iMac, he berated his good friend and ad partner Lee Clow over the phone. Jobs said Clow's team was getting the color wrong for the print ads. He shouted, "You guys don't know what you're doing. I'm going to get someone else to do the ads because this is fucked up."

> Eventually Clow sat Jobs down and made him look at the original photos versus print ads. Clow was right. Jobs backed down.

"This place sucks!"

> Former Chief Apple Designer Jony Ive went to the trouble of finding a boutique, 5-star hotel room for Jobs to stay at in London. As soon as Jobs got to his room he called up Ive and said, "I hate my room. It's a piece of shit, let's go." Jobs grabbed

his things to leave, stopping at the desk to tell the clerk what he thought of the hotel.

"Your smoothie sucks!"

Jony Ive tells this story: "Once we went to Whole Foods market to get a smoothie ... And this older woman was making it and he really got on her about how she was doing it." Jobs later felt bad realizing she's an older woman doing a job that she's not happy at.

"Everything you've ever done in your life is shit!"

The Xerox Star was supposed to be the hot new computer that came out in 1981 (it was ultimately a flop). Jobs and his team went to go check it out, but were unimpressed. A few weeks later he called Bob Belleville, one of the hardware designers on the Xerox Star team. "Everything you've ever done in your life is shit," Jobs said, "so why don't you come work for me?"

Belleville joined the team.

When His Parents Dropped Him Off at College, He Never Said Goodbye

[When his parents dropped him off] he refrained from even saying good-bye or thanks. He recounted the moment later with uncharacteristic regret: "It's one of the things in life I really feel ashamed about. I was not very sensitive, and I hurt their feelings. I shouldn't have. They had done so much to make sure I could go there, but I just didn't want them around. I didn't want anyone to know I had parents. I wanted to be like an orphan who had bummed around the country on trains and just arrived out of nowhere, with no roots, no connections, no background."

He Fired People Without Notice

When Steve had to make cutbacks at Pixar, he fired people and didn't give any severance pay. Pamela Kerwin, an early Pixar employee, pleaded that employees at least be given two weeks notice.

"Okay," he said, "but the notice is retroactive from two weeks ago."

He Would Harass People Interviewing for Work

"How old were you when you lost your virginity?" he asked. Th candidate looked baffled. "What did you say?" "Are you a virgin?" Jobs asked. The candidate sat there flustered, so Jobs changed the subject. "How many times have you taken LSD?" Hertzfeld recalled, "The poor guy was turning varying shades o red, so I tried to change the subject and asked a straightforward technical question." But when the candidate droned on in his response, Jobs broke in. "Gobble, gobble, gobble, gobble," he said, cracking up Smith and Hertzfeld. "I guess I'm not the righ guy," the poor man said as he got up to leave.

Fired Guy in Charge of MobileMe in Front of Employees.

When MobileMe launched in the summer of 2008, it was plagued with problems. People had trouble getting their data to sync to the cloud and across their devices.

The press, including the WSJ's Apple enthusiast Walt Mossberg slammed MobileMe as an unfinished product.

To address the problem, Jobs gathered the MobileMe team in Apple's auditorium and asked: "Can anyone tell me what MobileMe is supposed to do?" When the team gave their answers, Jobs replied, "Then why the fuck doesn't it do that?"

Jobs then fired the MobileMe boss on the spot and replaced hin with Eddie Cue.

Called Joe Nocera of The New York Times to Chew Him Out

In 2008, Joe Nocera was working on a column about Steve Jobs' health, criticizing Jobs and Apple for keeping it a secret from investors.

Before the column was published, Jobs called Nocera and said: "You think I'm an arrogant asshole who thinks he's above the law, and I think you're a slime bucket who gets most of his facts wrong."

Why was Jobs Such a Rude Person?

Isaacson asked Jobs' best friend Jony Ive what he thought. Here's his response:

> I once asked him why he gets so mad about stuff. He said, "But I don't stay mad." He has this very childish ability to get really worked up about something, and it doesn't stay with him at all. But, there are other times, I think honestly, when he's very frustrated, and his way to achieve catharsis is to hurt somebody. And I think he feels he has a liberty and license to do that. The normal rules of social engagement, he feels, don't apply to him. Because of how very sensitive he is, he knows exactly how to efficiently and effectively hurt someone. And he does do that.

Chapter 18
Purpose of Good Fucking Manners

It's to help you get ahead in life. To get ahead, you must repel those who aren't going anywhere or are sinking. To repel them, you must have manners different from theirs and similar to those you want to be. You are who you spend the most time with.

Do you want to be Elon Musk or a Trader Joe's cashier? Taylor Swift or a receptionist? Gordon Ramsey or a fast-food line cook? How does Steve Jobs act? How about the receptionist? What's the difference?

Perhaps not knowing the difference is why Americans who grew up lower-middle and middle class are miserable and angry. While they were encouraged to dream big as kids, they were taught the wrong manners needed to make it big. All the "please" and "thank you"s uttered and praised have been for naught. (So they turn to Socialism).

Those who know the difference (sometimes the middle and usually the upper-middle classes) say that they don't want to be assholes like Elon Musk, that it isn't worth it. That's fine, just don't think you're a better person than him. He produces results that benefit humanity while the nice guy pats himself on the back for not insulting his waitress after she fucks up his order. Voting for universal health care means jack shit compared to creating technology that makes universal health care possible and at a lower cost. Some want tangible results, not random acts of niceness.

To get ahead in life, you need good mental health. Does worrying about other people's feelings contribute to better mental health, or does it make worrier more anxious? Does lying about how you feel – "I'm fine, thanks you" – actually make you feel "fine" when you're anything but? Or is the obligatory lying emotionally draining and make you wonder why you're not as happy as other people say they are?

What have "good manners" gotten us?

Not social harmony or good health or any significant advances in society. Dictums like "don't hurt other people's feelings" have brought unprecedented censorship, anxiety, and shit-slinging. Mental health and educational standards have been getting worse ever since the self-esteem movement told everyone that they're perfect as is and don't need to change if they don't want to. "Respect" and "consideration" have turned into a confusing and divisive array of identify politics and safe spaces. Manners have consequences and whoever invented "good manners" can go fuck themselves.

"Good manners" isn't about creating a harmonious society or respecting people – what prevailing American etiquette experts say it's about -- it's about forcing people to learn arbitrary and asinine social formulas that protect feckless whiners and narcissistic dipshits from feeling like the piece of shit they are while making useless people feel good about themselves. These so-called etiquette experts also assume that we can make society and people better if they're educated on proper etiquette. Sounds like brainwashing, genteel bullying and moral grandstanding. It's "slave morality," as Friedrich Nietzsche puts it.

Nietzsche's concept of slave morality (aka victim morality) refers to an etiquette system created by dipshits who think they're hot shit but lack the will to back that up so they take down those who live the life they want to live. It's "crab mentality," where any crab that tries to escape from the pot gets pulled back down by other crabs.[27] These douchebags

[27] From: https://www.omaritani.com/blog/the-crab-mentality#:~:text=A%20crab%20placed%20alone%20in,and%20the%20group's%20collective%20demise.

create an etiquette system that labels anyone they feel inferior to as greedy and selfish oppressors who lack kindness, empathy, and compassion. They also emphasize equality, as in equality of access to resources, regardless of individual track record of handling resources.

In contrast, Nietzsche's master morality (aka noble morality) is based one's ability to overcome obstacles, to not care about what others think of you, and to pursue one's own interests without feeling guilty or ashamed. It's focused on making the self-stronger rather than making others weaker so you can feel better about yourself.

The resentful seek to turn the virtues of the weak into universal moral standards. Nietzsche believed that this leads to a cultural decline in which creativity, individualism, and the pursuit of excellence are devalued in favor of mediocrity and conformity. Sounds like the current fetish for the equality of outcomes.

Grumpy English professor Paul Fussell said, "If you find an American who feels entirely class-secure, stuff and exhibit him. He's a rare specimen."[28]
Obsession with class and good breeding is American society's dirty secret, that's why Americans are uniquely obsessed with etiquette books and

---

"A crab placed alone in a bucket will easily climb out and escape, but when you place it with a few of its mates, this interesting phenomenon occurs: One at a time, as the crabs try to escape, other crabs will pull them back down to their misery and the group's collective demise.

In psychology, this behavior became known as "The Crab Effect," or "The Crab Mentality," as a way to illustrate the selfish, harmful, and jealous mindset of some members in a group, who will try to undermine and halt the progress of the other better-performing members in the group."

[28] Paul Fussell: *Class: A Guide Through the American Status System*, all editions.

come up with elaborate rules of social engagement. Americans would lik[e] to believe that they've created a society where class doesn't matter, that they've moved beyond British cultural norms. Yet class matters as much in the US as it does in the UK especially to the lower-middle and middle classes who can't figure out why they're stuck. Just because Americans don't have the titles the British have doesn't mean rigid class divisions don't exist in the US. Class status and consciousness is signaled more subtly, that's all. The lower middle-class woman with a Sociology degree from a bullshit university is signaling that she's moved up from her degreeless parents when she uses words like "intersectionality" and "heteronormative" in an argument with them, even though financially sh[e] hasn't and will probably die poorer than them. Good manners is bullshi[t] it doesn't make people's lives better, it only makes the prideful and envious feel better about themselves. Good manners is a dangerous mix of leftie egalitarian cultural politics and ideological elitism. It's as if Ayn Rand becomes a Communist, psycho-bitches are everywhere.

Good Fucking Manners

Good fucking manners cuts through the slave/victim morality bullshit and asks what works for you so you can live a healthy and fulfilling life. These manners aren't drawn from the advice actions of the American "upper class" – those who attended exclusive East Coast boarding school[s] and colleges. They're compiled from experience and reading about how elite performers act and think. Some, like Bill Gates, came from upper class families. Steve Jobs came from the lower-middle class, a carpenter father and homemaker mother who couldn't afford his private college tuition, he dropped out after one semester at Reed College. High school drop-out Marco Pierre White grew up poor, neglected, and hungry enough that he scavenged for food. Taylor Swift grew up upper-middle class.

Regardless of how and where they grew up, the only thing that matters about them is their success and what they've done to achieve it. This gets the reader away from the self-limiting thinking that success is a function of class. Success here is instead understood as a function of how one treats oneself and others. The only thing that matters here is success, not "respect for others," (whatever that means), especially when I've never met someone who respects everyone equally and I don't see why anyone should. Yet something tells me that the single-minded focus on personal success leads to more respectful treatment of people than expected. Fat people who preach "body positivity" will shame Adele for losing 100 pounds, but I've yet to have seen a fit person do the same to a fat person at the gym.

So practice *good manners* if you want to be liked by a bunch of people who aren't going anywhere in life, who work for vacation and retirement. If you aspire for more, have *good fucking manners.*

Chapter 19
Suggested Readings

It's not true that only women read and write etiquette books. It's that etiquette books written by men are labeled otherwise, either as self-help or as philosophy. Robert Greene's *48 Laws of Power* and *The Art of Seduction* fall under the self-help instead of etiquette genre and its readers are mostly men. Friedrich Nietzsche's *Human All Too Human: A Book for Free Spirits* is a philosophical text that's actually an etiquette book. Here's an aphorism from the book that's etiquette advice: "He who cannot put his thoughts on ice should not enter into the heat of dispute," which sounds like something Miss Manners has said. While I consider Paul Fussell's *Class: A Guide Through America's Status System* as an anthropological work written by an English professor, it too can be read as an etiquette guide. He does, after all, tell you how to respond to dumb questions without being rude and tells you why it's a lame idea to advertise where your kid goes to college on your car. In fact, the appendix of Fussell's *Class...* is written in standard etiquette form, where he answers questions about proper etiquette.

We'll get to these etiquette books later. First, let's pay homage to the classics of American etiquette so we can better understand American manners of the present.

The Classics

They're worth reading, they're usually not vapid. They're written by women who grew up upper-middle to upper class and attended elite school institutions such as Wellesley College and Packer Collegiate Institute. The most prominent among them are Emily Post, Amy Vanderbilt, and Miss Manners, aka Judith Martin. They all asserted that etiquette isn't a fixed set of rules and rituals and must adapt to changing times and different cultural contexts. They emphasized treating others with respect, consideration, and kindness, regardless of their social status, background, or beliefs. They believed that good manners and gracious behavior were not just a form of decorum, but a way of expressing one's inner values and character. They focused on putting other people at ease more than on personal success and it's implied that good manners will result in personal success.

Their popularity during the 20th century suggests that 20th century Americans understood etiquette as social access to those with good breeding (the upper class, the right schools). And that's probably still the case today, year 2023, because I hear a lot about first-generation college kids who return home and think they're better than their parents. Colleges continue to function as finishing schools for young adults, teaching them what to say and think to appear enlightened, fashionable, and intelligent.

Suggested readings:

- Emily Post's Etiquette (19 editions)
- Amy Vanderbilt Complete Book of Etiquette (3 editions)
- Miss Manner's Guide to Excruciating Correct Behavior

Samples from Emily Post (1872-1960, her progeny continue to update her work)

She was popular with upper middle-class women. She didn't care about trifling details such as which fork to use (she says it doesn't matter to those in high positions so it shouldn't matter to anyone). She was focused on getting shit done efficiently, effectively, and fairly. Example:

Email Manners
   1. Always Respond

Junk mail and forwards are one thing, but you should always respond to a real message, whether it's to invite you to a meeting or a party or a hello from an old friend. Make it a goal to respond within 24 hours.

2. What's the Story?

Don't keep your readers in suspense. Use the Subject line to alert the receiver to the subject matter of your message—you're likely to get a faster response.

3. Addresses Ad-nauseum.

When sending out an email to a long list of recipients, consider using an address book function that doesn't list all recipients in the "to" header. Having to scroll past a long list of addresses to get to the message itself is annoying. Plus, many people may not like having their email address displayed to others.

4. Rapid Fire Responses

If you only check your email once a week, let people know. Otherwise, they may take offense at not receiving a timely (which when it comes to email can mean immediate) response from you. On the other hand, don't hit the rapid response button when you're hot under the collar. Let your email simmer—overnight if necessary— and re-read it when you've calmed down. Then, decide to edit or delete.

I imagine Post as my mother whenever I read her books.

Amy Vanderbilt (1908-1974)

The least intelligent and intellectual of the three listed above, she was popular with middlebrow women with Cinderella fantasies. Her advice is more detailed than analytical – which fork to use, how to act at dinner table -- and she tends to follow traditions for the sake of following them instead of asking if they deserve to exist. Sample advice she gives:

> *Tasting Another's Food*
> Sometimes a couple dining in a restaurant wish to taste each other's food. This is informal but permissible, though only if a fresh fork or spoon is used, with the possessor of the dish then handing the "taste" implement, handle first, to the other person. The other must not reach across the table and eat from a companion's plate, no matter how many years they have been married. If one of the two has had included some item say French fried potatoes in his order and doesn't wish them, he asks the waiter to serve them to the other, if desired he doesn't take them on his plate, then re-serve them.

If Vanderbilt were my mom, I'd throw my dinner at her and take a piss on hers.

Miss Manners, Judith Martin (1938-present [2023])

The most philosophically robust and snarky of the three, she's in her 80s and still (2023) giving etiquette advice and making snide observations about the state of American society. She hates rudeness, emphasizes the need for restraint, and focuses on awkward situations, like how to respond to rude behavior from other people. Example from a column published in several media outlets on February 19, 2022:

> DEAR MISS MANNERS: I have a colleague who continues to forget my name and who I am, especially when we are in a large group situation. At a conference, he will say to me, "I don't think we've met; who are you?", even though we've met several times before.

127

Not wanting to be rude, I respond, "I'm sorry, my name is ..." to his smug face. Other colleagues have warned me that he uses this ploy on them, as well, for his self-amusement and to appear superior. It's as if to say, "You didn't leave much of an impression on me the last time we met."

I know Miss Manners disapproves of responding to rudeness with rudeness, but does she have any suggestion on how to handle this situation?

GENTLE READER: Since he clearly enjoys amusement, Miss Manners suggests that you indulge him: "Oh Kevin, you trickster. It's me, Pradeep. The one whose office is right next to yours?" Then add, to the others nearby, "I just hope he doesn't pull that with our clients, or we'll all be in trouble!"

Touché, Miss Manners. Here's an example of her intellectual prowess when writing about the role of etiquette in society:

Class Consciousness
There are three social classes in America upper-middle class, middle-class and lower-middle class. Miss Manners has never heard of an American owning up to be any other class. [Not true, lots of lower-middle and middle-class Socialists identify as poor]. However, if there's one thing that all Americans can agree upon no matter what their background, it is that the middle-class is despicable. [
The shame of having been born into it is sufficient excuse for a lifelong grudge against one's parents and the entire society. This is not a happy state-of-affairs.

The problem, in Miss Manner's opinion, is that the classes have traditionally behaved badly either oppressively or obsequiously to those below or above them. Being in the middle, the middle class has the opportunity to do both. Being a democracy, we extend this opportunity to everyone.

Miss Manners is the rudest and most insightful of the Classics, and that's why she's fun to read and probably a good lay.

Queertiquette

Fashionable women throughout the 20th century always had gay friends, especially male ones because they were considered to be the best arbiters of good taste and manners and could be counted on to be honest to women due to their lack of sexual interest in them. Gay men's reputation as dandies continues in the 21st century, most notably displayed on hit show, *Queer Eye for the Straight Guy* (2003-2007, 2018-present), where gay men give straight men (and an occasional woman) a makeover, from clothes to décor to everyday manners.

Quentin Crisp (1908-1999)

From the 1970s until his death in 1999, Quentin Crisp was America's favorite flaming fag due to his outrageous personality, flamboyant fashion sense, and astute wit. He had roles in several films, including as Elizabeth I in *Orlando* (1992), was a guest on David Letterman (1982-1983), and the subject of Sting's song, an *Englishman in New York*.

Despite being born to a middle-class family, Crisp wasn't a proponent of etiquette, which he sees as a "class system based on snobbery and exclusion." He instead focuses on style and manners, "the means of getting what you want without appearing to be an absolute swine." To that end, the mildly misanthropic Crisp extols the art of euphemism and the virtue of the lie -- "the basic building blocks of good manners." People "should never be asked to put up with our natural selves or see us as we really are, ever!"

129

Good style, however, is a matter of personal integrity. That is, the refusal to conform to fashion – "groupspeak," Crisp calls it. It's okay to lie to others to keep them happy, but it's not okay to lie to or about oneself regarding one's own desires. "A stylist neither copies nor competes."[29]

Crisp's style is minimalistic, he believes that less is best because people don't give a shit about your problems and saying too much will get you in trouble. Among subjects he advises stylists to avoid include:

- Personal disasters
- Your sex life
- Your past
- The flaws of others
- Any subject on which your opinion is too eagerly solicited.

This list that makes me wonder if there's anything left to talk about if we were all be become Crisperanto stylists. Might we become mutes if we can't talk shit about other people and our latest sexual exploits?

Suggested Readings:

- *Manners from Heaven: A Divine Guide to Good Behavior* (1985)
- *Doing it with Style* (1981, with Donald Carroll)

Quotes:

- Fashion is what you adopt when you don't know who you are.
- I recommend limiting one's involvement in other people's lives to a pleasantly scant minimum.

---

[29] Pg. 9, from *Doing it with Style* (1981), by Quentin Crisp and Donald Carroll.

- There is no need to do any housework at all. After the first four years the dirt doesn't get any worse.
- Never keep up with the Joneses. Drag them down to your level.
- Aesthetic considerations aside, both jargon and slang have two drawbacks, either of which would be sufficient to disqualify them from having any place in the vocabulary of a stylist. The first is that both are forms of groupspeak, and someone with style shuns identification with a group. (Doing it with Style)
- Euphemisms are unpleasant truths wearing diplomatic cologne. (Manners)

Florence King (1936-2016)

A pornographer, essayist, misanthropist, conservative, lesbian, and elitist, Florence King was born into a lower-middle class Southern family whose grandmother believed was upper-class by lineage. Hilarity ensues when that happens, especially since King wanted to be a boy/man instead of the Southern Belle her grandmother expected her to be. She had a column for the National Review called "The Misanthrope's Corner" and was nicknamed "The Queen of Mean." "I don't suffer fools," she once told an interviewer, "and I like to see fools suffer."

Straight men were especially intimidated by her, possibly because she hated effeminate men and any hint of femininity she found in a man she'd ~~castrate~~ castigate. She never wrote a formal etiquette book, but her focus on the whys and wherefores of manners, especially Southern ones, means her books can be read as one.

Suggested Reading:

- *Confessions of a Failed Southern Lady: A Memoir (1990)*

Quotes:

- A man should never apologize!
- You can't pretend to be witty because wit is dry, subtle, lacerating, cynical, elitist, and risque - all impossible to fake. Humor, on the other hand, is broad, soothing, positive, inclusive, and smutty - to make sure everybody gets it. Pretending to be humorous is easy, and a great many people are doing it.
- The witty woman is a tragic figure in American life. Wit destroys eroticism and eroticism destroys wit, so women must choose between taking lovers and taking no prisoners.
- A professional bitch does the Southern man proud. If she is skittish, high-strung, and easily upset, that means she is a thoroughbred with good blood as opposed to a sluggish peasant.
- For a woman who does not know whether to be hot or cold, temper tantrums are a convenient compromise. Men find it very easy to translate female rage into female genital rage. She indeed looks mighty pretty when she's mad; her cheeks flame, her eyes glitter, and she trembles uncontrollably. It looks like an orgasm.

Etiquette to Piss off Basic Bitches

These books aren't considered etiquette books, but they should. Some of Robert Greene's books provide as much detail about how one should handle oneself in situations as typical etiquette books. Paul Fussell's anthropological analysis of class consciousness in America is the same.

Paul Fussell

Born into an upper-middle class family, Fussell graduated from Pomona College (elite liberal arts school) and received his PhD in English Literature from Harvard University. Afterwards, he spent most of his academic career at Rutgers and University of Pennsylvania. Prior to his graduate studies, he served in the armed forces during World War II, and was awarded a Purple Heart.

Fussell had a critical and satirical approach to etiquette. He thinks etiquette has more to do with ridiculous social yearnings and class consciousness than promoting civility, as the Classic have it. The middle-class, for instance, act as they think those above them act to create an artificial sense of superiority, with dreadful consequences. So Fussell uses rapierlike observations and satire to subvert and undermine social norms and courtesies sacred to Basic Bitches.

Suggested readings:

- Class: A Guide Through America's Class System (1983)
- BAD: or the Dumbing of America (1991)

Here are some samples from *Class: A Guide Through America's Class System*:

- Americans are the only people in the world known to me whose status anxiety prompts them to advertise their college and university affiliations in the rear window of their automobiles.
- Say "motherfucker" at least once a day.
- The middles cleave to euphemisms not just because they're an aid in avoiding facts. They like them also because they assist their social yearnings towards pomposity. This is possible because most euphemisms permit the speaker to multiply syllables, and the middle class confuses sheer numerousness with weight and value.
- Anybody who notices unpleasant facts in the have-a-nice-day world we live in is going to be designated a curmudgeon.

In contrast to Quentin Crisp's embrace of euphemisms to promote civility, Fussell is appalled by them. The consequences of lying, he argue, is far worse than the fleeting feel-good moments afforded by euphemistic language. For Fussell, well-mannered people are always honest without regard to other people's feelings.

Samples from *BAD: or the Dumbing of America*:

- BAD is something phony, clumsy, witless, untalented, vacant, o boring that many Americans can be persuaded is genuine, graceful, bright, or fascinating.

- Thus, BAD. The United States especially overflows with it because of all countries it is the most addicted to self-praise and complacency - even more than France.

Robert Greene (1959-Present)

Greene had an "insanely middle-class" upbringing in Los Angeles. His father sold cleaning supplies while his mother was a housewife with thwarted artistic ambitions. Greene attended UC Berkeley and graduate from University of Wisconsin, Madison with a degree in Classics. His reading of the classics of social and political thought is the basis of his books.

While Greene's books – most are New York Times bestsellers -- are published not as etiquette books, but under the rubric of self-help, they read like a standard etiquette book. They include, for instance, detailed analysis of how a historical figure handled a situation and its consequences. The main difference between Greene and most of the other etiquette experts listed in this chapter, is that he's focused on personal growth and success rather than civility and social harmony. Tha might be why some of his books are banned in certain US prisons and have been described as a handbook for psychopaths.

Greene's books are among some of the most popular in US prisons. They're also popular with prominent music artists, CEOs, and politicians, including 50 Cent, Drake, Kanye West, Michael Jackson, Courtney Love, Dov Charney (former CEO of American Apparel), and Fidel Castro. References to Greene's most seminal and most controversial work, *The 48 Laws of Power* have been made in numerous rap songs.

Suggested Readings:

- 48 Laws of Power
- Art of Seduction

Some highlights from *48 Laws of Power*:

- Never assume that the person you are dealing with is weaker or less important than you are. Some people are slow to take offense, which may make you misjudge the thickness of their skin, and fail to worry about insulting them. But should you offend their honor and their pride, they will overwhelm you with a violence that seems sudden and extreme given their slowness to anger. If you want to turn people down, it is best to do so politely and respectfully, even if you feel their request is impudent or their offer ridiculous.
- Lord, protect me from my friends; I can take care of my enemies.
- ...person who cannot control his words shows that he cannot control himself, and is unworthy of respect.
- **Always Say Less Than Necessary**
  When you are trying to impress people with words, the more you say, the more common you appear, and the less in control. Even if you are saying something banal, it will seem original if you

make it vague, open-ended, and sphinxlike. Powerful people impress and intimidate by saying less. The more you say, the more likely you are to say something foolish."

Highlights from the *Art of Seduction*, an etiquette book in which Greene instructs you to first rid yourself of your anti-seductive qualities:

- Niceness in seduction, however, though it may at first draw someone to you (it is soothing and comforting), soon loses all effect. Being too nice can literally push the target away from you. Erotic feeling depends on the creation of tension. Without tension, without anxiety and suspense, there can be no feeling of release, of true pleasure and joy.
- Charmers. First, they don't talk much about themselves, which heightens their mystery and disguises their limitations. Second, they seem to be interested in us, and their interest is so delightfully focused that we relax and open up to them. Finally, Charmers are pleasant to be around. They have none of most people's ugly qualities—nagging, complaining, self-assertion. They seem to know what pleases.
- Never whine, never complain, never try to justify yourself.

Friedrich Nietzsche (1844-1900)

While Nietzsche, born to a middle-class family, is known as a philosopher, he can be read as a cranky etiquette expert who thinks of manners and morals not in terms of good and bad, but as the struggle between the "will to power," – the desire to live instinctively – and socially approved behavior.

Nietzsche was an elitist. His concept of the noble (master) and victim (slave) moralities refers to two opposing ethical systems. The noble morality is characterized by strength, individualism, and a will to power.

In this system, individuals create their own values and are willing to take risks to achieve their goals. In contrast, the victim morality is characterized by weakness, conformity, and a focus on the needs of others, such as how people want to be addressed. In this system, individuals don't create their own values but instead adopt the values of the group to which they belong. Moored in groupthink, they are more concerned with avoiding punishment than achieving success.

Nietzsche believed that victim morality seeks to undermine noble morality. Victim morality is based on resentment of and a desire for revenge against the successful and free rather than desire to make the world better. This worldview means there'll always be two competing etiquette systems, one focused on the taming of the instinctive self, the other on achieving success through courage and ambition.

Suggested readings:

- *Human, All Too Human: A Book for Free Spirits* (1878)
- *Beyond Good and Evil: Prelude to a Philosophy of the Future* (1886)
- *On the Genealogy of Morals: a Polemic* (1887)

Highlights from *Human, All Too Human*

- He is called a free spirit who thinks differently from what, on the basis of his origin, environment, his class and profession, or on the basis of the dominant views of the age, would have been expected of him.
- Stupidity in a woman is unfeminine.
- In reality, hope is the worst of all evils, because it prolongs man's torments.

From *Beyond Good and Evil*

- To talk much about oneself may also be a means of concealing oneself.
- Insanity in individuals is something rare—but in groups, parties, nations, and epochs it is the rule.
- Objection, evasion, joyous distrust, and love of irony are signs of health; everything absolute belongs to pathology.

From *On the Genealogy of Morals*

- ...'I suffer: someone or other must be guilty' – and every sick sheep thinks the same.
- The sick are the greatest danger for the healthy; it is not from the strongest that harm comes to the strong, but from the weakest.
- The slave revolt in morality begins when 'ressentiment' itself becomes creative and gives birth to values: the ressentiment of natures that are denied the true reaction, that of deeds, and compensate themselves with an imaginary revenge. While every noble morality develops from a triumphant affirmation of itself, slave morality from the outset says No to what is "outside," what is "different," what is "not itself"; and this No is its creative deed.

Chapter 20
Final Thoughts and Questions

Americans and other culturally Anglo nations seem to be uniquely obsessed with rudeness. They don't want to be considered rude and they have a habit of calling out rudeness and those they don't like rude. They'll say:

- "Well, that's rude!"
- "I don't mean to be rude, but…"
- "Don't be rude!"
- "Omigod, she's like, sooo rude."
- "Awww, you're so polite!" (the opposite of rude)

Meanwhile, I've never heard a French, Chinese, or Mexican person call someone rude. (Readers, correct me if I'm wrong, email is foodyap@gmail.com). The closet word to rude in French is "grossier," and that translates more closely as "coarse and unrefined" rather than "ill-mannered and disrespectful," which I take as the meaning of rude in the mainstream American context. In the US, I'm frequently called rude, check my Google and Yelp reviews (Alive Juice Bar or The Soup Nazi Kitchen) for instances. Growing up Chinese, I was never called rude, only a "naughty ghost" and "lazy and stupid," the latter which would be considered rude and unacceptable in the present US cultural milieu. Americans often refer to French and Chinese service as rude, yet the reverse doesn't happen. It's not that the French and Chinese don't have etiquette, they, and I suppose all societies, do. Rules of conduct must exist for there to be coherence in everyday transactions. So one of my aims here is to figure out why Americans are obsessed with rudeness, and by extension, etiquette.

To begin with, why are there so many etiquette books coming out of the UK and the US? Why are there etiquette columns in US newspapers but none in French and Chinese ones that I know of? Why were etiquette schools so popular in the Anglo 20ᵗʰ century (they're now considered outdated, but a few still exist). What's the meaning of the decline in popularity of etiquette schools? Why are the only etiquette schools I can find in China are those specializing in international business and Anglo (British especially) manners? Why can't I find one etiquette school in China that focuses on Chinese manners?

Behind every obsession is something sinister, a hidden dysfunction that leads to more dysfunction. Might that dysfunction be narcissism, the deadliest of the deadly sins? In America, one can be considered polite and well-bred as long as "thank yous" and "pleases" are said with frequency. Meanwhile, all sorts of time-wasting and preening behavior either go unnoticed or are perversely recognized as good and genteel behavior. The resulting dissonance that happens when outward displays of "good manners" are used to conceal one's inward corruption is the source of America's struggle with batshit crazy. That's the thesis of this book -- people go crazy when their sense of self doesn't match up with who they really are. Americans are the ostrich, American manners, the sand. There's a pack of hyenas nearby.

Why do you follow etiquette? Is it slavish devotion to a famous name, like Vanderbilt or the British royal family? (Consider the popularity of Downton Abbey for its ostentatious displays of ridiculous good manners). To get shit done, as Emily Post has it and like the Chinese who take courses on international business etiquette? To put rude people who pretend to be genteel in their place, as Miss Manners does?

Or do you reject etiquette, as Quintin Crisp does? Do you consider it as socially acceptable bullying, as Crisp and Paul Fussell do? Has mainstream American etiquette become slavish, celebrating victimhood and the weak-willed, as Nietzsche saw it happen in his version of the history of the West? Where has American etiquette taken us? (And by "us," I don't mean just the US, but the world because of the potency of American cultural capital). Is the ongoing American obsession with etiquette the reason why Americans are so preoccupied with pronouns and other identity related naming conventions?

Do you respect everyone equally? Should you?

About the Author

He's lived in the Seattle metro area since 2001. He grew up in Taiwan, the US, and Singapore. He went to a fancy East Coast boarding school. He went to a fancy college too. He got kicked out of the PhD program in Anthropology at the University of Washington for mocking Woke dipshits. Yelp, Craigslist, Quora have banned him, and he's shadow banned on Facebook. He's owned Alive Juice Bar since 2010 and The Soup Nazi Kitchen since 2020, both located in downtown Everett, WA. Antifa has shot at him. Routinely he receives hate mail and occasionally, a death threat. He writes a weekly comic strip titled The Misadventures of Dipshit Doug Evans, you can find it on Alive Juice Bar's Instagram and YouTube pages. He often craves Taiwanese stinky tofu, Hong Kong style congee, and Shanghai soup dumplings. He owned a Siberian Husky named Chinook. He wants an Australian Shepherd and name her Emay. He wants to do yoga with her.

What's Been Said About Author

"Rude...rude rude rude!

"Pretentious prick..."

"Arrogant asshole."

"...one of the most difficult personalities in the Puget Sound region."

"That guy Andrew, he's an evil man!"

"Andrew...you are batshit crazy."

"...he's PSYCHO. If you're reading this, get some help!"

"The owner is not a lot of warm and fuzzy."

.

Upcoming Books By This Author

White, Whiney, and Woke: The New Face of the KKK (Winter 2023)

Wonder why most who identify as Woke are White? Is it possible for someone with a name like Doug Evans be Jewish? What do the Woke think about while they're taking a shit? What is Woke sex like? Do Woke men have small dicks? Read this book to find out how the KKK has morphed into the Woke and what their daily lives are like. This book also explores the philosophical underpinnings of Woke lifestyle and ideology, like why they're obsessed with pronouns and Woke concepts such as intersectionality. Read this book if you dare to look at the darkest side of humanity.

How to Suck Your Own Dick: an Alive Juice Bar's Guide to Men's Health (Spring 2024)

Imagine the body of a man who can suck his own dick. Is he fat? What size is his dick? How limber is he?

The ability to suck your own dick is the ultimate marker of a man's health and virility. A man who can must be in excellent shape and the goal of this book is to train you to reach the pinnacle of men's health. Nutrition, exercises, mindset, and daily routine are some of the topics that will be discussed.

146

Other Books By This Author

How to Eat Like an Asshole

Do YOU eat like an asshole? How do you know if you eat like an asshole? Do you eat things that make you look like an asshole without realizing it? The Juice Nazi — owner of Alive Juice Bar, located in a Seattle suburb — mercilessly dissects American dining etiquette and American manners in general to reveal cultural idiosyncrasies many don't notice. This book explains why what's typically considered as elegant and graceful, as good manners and fine taste, are actually signs of stupidity and depravity. This book will make those who consider themselves part of the American middle-class in manners and morals, squirm.

I'm Just Not That Kind of Girl: a sadistic basic bitch story

Roxanne G. is trying to get her boyfriend — Dummy Boy — to tattoo her name on his penis. He doesn't want to do that. So Roxanne uses her womanly wiles to train Dummy Boy to do what he doesn't want to do — go to a bookstore and hot yoga, eat sushi and dim sum, attend a symphony and book reading...until he finally agrees to get the tattoo. She dumps him after he gets it, leaving him distraught and suicidal. Read this misandristic story to find out if Dummy Boy survives to show his penis to another woman.

How to Go to School Like an Asian

Curious about homeschooling? Ever fantasized about swapping your kid for an Asian one, even if the Asian is a paraplegic? Want to be Asian at school so you can win all sorts of awards, build robots named Tiffany, and get rejected by Harvard and Princeton but accepted at Caltech? Did you write hate mail to Tiger Mom Cunt, Amy Chua? Then this is the book on education for you! The notorious Juice Nazi is back and ready to read your hate mail and death threats with his most offensive and triggering book since the banned-on Amazon cookbook, *How to Cook Like a Racist.* Here he breezily explains why Asians as the model minority isn't a myth, it's for real; why Filipinos, Indonesians, Thais, and Malaysians aren't Asian unless they're ethnically Chinese. And why it's better to commit suicide as a teenager than to become a lifelong heroin addict. As a bonus, there are 20 exercises — lots of Math, of course — you can do to help you go to school like an Asian. Ching Chong!

Paradise Frost: Satan as Santa

Think Hell is hot? Think again, it's as frigid as Mother Theresa. John Milton wrote the literary classic *Paradise Lost* to give us Satan's perspective of his predicament and The Fall of humankind. Dante Aligheri wrote *The Inferno,* part one of his *Divine Comedies,* to give us a look at life in Hell. When you combine the two and set Hell on the North Pole, you get *Paradise Frost: Satan as Santa.* Read it to learn how much of a sinner you are. Read it to be surprised by who is stuck in Hell. Read it to find out how the deviant Mrs. Clause uses her elves as dildos. Read it to discover how Santa satisfies his carnal urges with human whores. Read it to decide if this is a work of blasphemy.

Made in the USA
Las Vegas, NV
29 June 2023

74034369R00085